Alfred's LEARN TO PLAY Blues Guitar

The Easiest Way to Play the Blues

Steve Trovato
Terry Carter

Alfred Music Publishing Co., Inc.
P.O. Box 10003
Van Nuys, CA 91410-0003
alfred.com

ISBN-10: 0-7390-9531-5 (Book & DVD)
ISBN-13: 978-0-7390-9531-7 (Book & DVD)

Cover photos
Guitar: Fender®, Stratocaster®, and the distinctive headstock design commonly found on the Strat® guitar are registered trademarks of Fender Musical Instruments Corporation and used herein with express written permission. All rights reserved.
Background: © iStockphoto/Boris Rabtsevich • © iStockphoto/Peter Zelei

Alfred Cares. Contents printed on 100% recycled paper.

Contents

About the DVD

A companion video, hosted by author Steve Trovato, is included with this book. The DVD features clear demonstrations of the lessons and music examples in this book. Watch it while following along with the book for the best learning experience.

The Blues Lead Guitar section of the DVD includes play-along MP3 accompaniment tracks for you to hone your skills as a blues lead guitarist.

DVD-ROM Audio Instructions

To access the MP3 accompaniment files for the Blues Lead Guitar section, place the disc in the DVD drive of your computer.

Windows users: double-click on My Computer, right-click on your DVD drive icon, select Explore, and then double-click on the DVD-ROM Materials folder.

Mac users: double-click on the DVD icon on your desktop, and then double-click on the DVD-ROM Materials folder.

Introduction

Welcome to *Alfred's Learn to Play Blues Guitar.* This simple, straightforward, and effective approach to learning to play blues guitar is intended for beginning to advanced guitarists looking to enhance their playing and repertoire with this unique style.

The book and companion video are organized into two main sections (Blues Rhythm Guitar and Blues Lead Guitar) to provide the foundation for learning authentic blues guitar. Start by learning over 50 blues rhythm patterns in a multitude of blues styles—including medium shuffle, uptown blues, slow blues, blues-rock, and mambo. The lead section features basic soloing techniques, such as slides, hammer-ons, pull-offs, bending, vibrato, rakes, and more. You will be diving right in by learning and playing 18 great blues solos in the styles of legends like Eric Clapton, Albert Collins, Jimi Hendrix, Stevie Ray Vaughan, Albert King, and B. B. King.

Guitarists using this book should already be familiar with basic guitar and music theory concepts. Before we start with the playing, we'll cover some of the foundations of the blues—including a brief history lesson and refreshers on blues form, blues rhythms, and tablature reading. Some of you might have this material down already, so consider it a review.

A Brief History of the Blues as a Style

When most people think of blues guitar we think of greats like Eric Clapton, B. B. King, Stevie Ray Vaughan, and Jimmy Page, but let's take a look back to the beginning to see where it all came from.

Blues guitar as a style is an outgrowth of the work song and field holler traditions of the African slaves at the turn of the 19th century—a period when Africans were captured and brought to America against their will. They were sold to plantation owners and put to work as common workers. One of their jobs was to clear land to prepare it for an incoming railroad system that was being built throughout the American south. Chained together in groups of four or five people, they would be brought to a location and made to work from dawn until dusk six days per week; their pay was about 25 cents a day.

Slaves were watched closely to prevent escape and were not permitted to speak because plantation owners feared escape plots would be hatched. They were however permitted to sing. To pass the time, slaves would sing for hours on end. Their work was hard and to conserve energy their songs needed to be short. They also followed the African tradition of *call and response,* singing back and forth to each other, usually with a leader singing a short phrase and a group answering it in unison. This call and response tradition became one of the backbones of the blues.

As new railroads began to cross the southern countryside, the field workers would hear the train wheels clacking over the gaps in the tracks. This sound was heard as a musical rhythm by early slave musicians who began using it as a rhythmic device in their songs. This rhythmic feel became what is known as the blues, or *shuffle,* feel today. This feel, along with call and response, is the essence of the blues. In this book, we will concentrate on these essential elements, examining how they are used in blues guitar playing.

Blues Form

The most common form of the blues is the *12-bar blues,* which is 12 measures (or bars) in length and mainly uses just three chords. These chords are built on the first (I), fourth (IV), and fifth (V) degrees of the major scale. Measures 1–4 are the one (I) chord, measures 5–6 are the four (IV) chord, and measures 7–8 go back to the one (I) chord. Measures 9–12 consist of the five (V) chord in measure 9, the four (IV) in measure 10, the one (I) chord in measure 11, and the five (V) chord in measure 12; this is also known as the *turnaround.* A turnaround is a short musical statement that points the listener back to the beginning. The chords are all usually dominant seventh chords unless the key is minor.

Although there are other blues forms, the 12-bar form is by far the most common. This book will cover various stylistic techniques within the 12-bar context. Here is an example of a 12-bar blues in E.

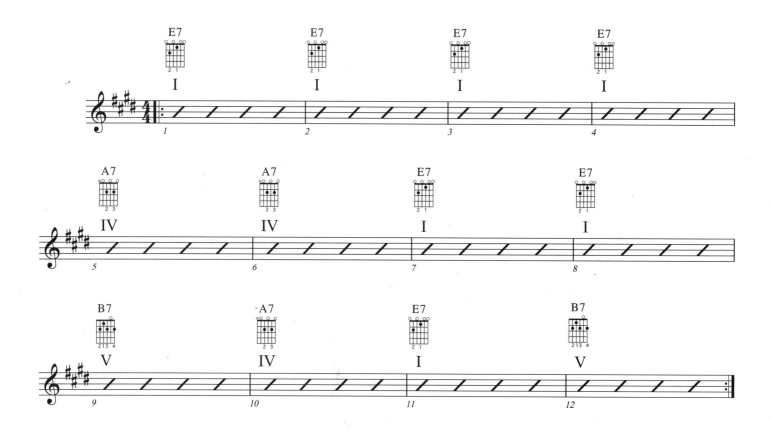

Blues Rhythm

The blues is frequently performed in a variety of tempos, keys, and rhythms. The feels fall primarily within four categories: 1) The shuffle (or swing), 2) the straight eighth-note feel, 3) the mambo, and 4) the slow blues $\frac{12}{8}$ feel. Most other blues feels are variations or permutations of these four basic rhythms.

Blues Phrasing

Phrasing is perhaps the most important aspect of blues guitar playing. The scales will tell you which notes to play, while phrasing will determine when and how to play them. Phrasing is the element of music that makes it sound like a given style. Rhythmic and melodic phrasing are essential to playing blues guitar because they outline, or describe, the underlying feel.

e familiar with the concept of call and response. To this day, nse in their blues soloing. It is a concept that will be demonstrated

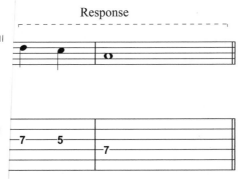

o play the blues is to break it down into measure subdivisions. ic theory in this book, but we will need to learn and understand

The *measure* is a musical ... a grouping of beats. In this book, we'll always divide the measure into four evenly spaced beats. Each of these beats is called a *quarter note*.

THE QUARTER NOTE

When you tap your foot along with the rhythm of a blues song, each tap of your foot counts as a beat. Four of these beats, or quarter notes, make up a measure. This is called $\frac{4}{4}$ time—meaning there are four beats to a measure and a quarter note gets one beat. These noteheads are solid and have a "stem" on them (see example below). If you strike each of these notes on the beat, you are playing quarter notes. Try playing only downstrokes [⊓] to feel the downbeat of each beat. In other words, you should pick notes using a downstroke as your foot hits the ground so that your pick and foot are moving in the same direction. If you play four quarter notes, you have played one measure of music in $\frac{4}{4}$ time.

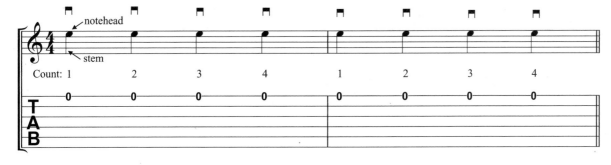

EIGHTH NOTES

Next, we have *eighth notes.* You will notice they have solid noteheads with stems attached at the bottom or top by beams. (Note: If an eighth note appears by itself, it has a flag at the end of the stem.) You should play each note with an alternating right-hand shuffle, or swing, feel (see below for explanation). The first eighth note is played with a downstroke and the second with an upstroke [∨] , and so on. The importance here is to understand that quarter notes are hit on the *downbeat* (numbered) while eighth notes are played on the *upbeat* (the "ands"). This means that a total of eight eighth notes can be played in every four-beat measure. As you tap your foot, play a note when your foot hits the floor and another when your foot reaches its highest point up. Do this four times and you will have played a measure of eighth notes. To get the notes evenly spaced across each beat, you could say "1-and, 2-and, 3-and, 4-and" (abbreviated 1+ 2+ 3+ 4+). Say the beat number when your foot hits the ground and say "and" ("+") when your foot is up.

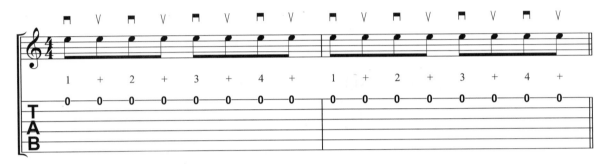

THE TRIPLET

The next essential rhythm is the *triplet,* which divides each beat into three equal parts. Triplets usually appear as three notes connected together with a line above them and a small number "3" above the line. There can be a total of four eighth-note triplet figures in each measure and each figure represents one beat. You can count 1-trip-let, 2-trip-let, etc. Here is what they look like.

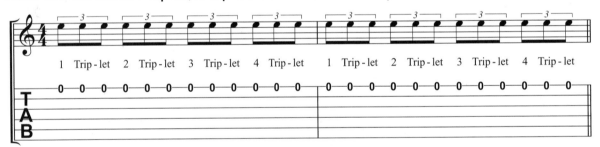

THE SHUFFLE FEEL

The *shuffle* feel is the backbone of blues rhythm and soloing, and it is essential to understand it before we proceed. Shuffle feel is derived from the eighth-note triplet. It is produced when you stop playing the middle syllable of an eighth-note triplet—you are left with only the first and last syllables. This will sound: 1 – let, 2 – let, 3 – let, 4 – let. We will learn how to translate this feel into blues phrasing on the guitar.

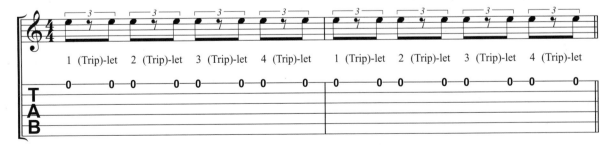

In this book, all music with the shuffle feel will have the indication (♩♩ = ♩ ♩) at the beginning of the piece.

How to Read Tablature (TAB)

Tablature, or TAB, is a valuable notational tool for reading and playing guitar music—it provides a visual snapshot of the six strings of the guitar. In TAB, notes and chords are indicated by the placement of the fret numbers on each string (which are all represented by a horizontal line). The following covers some of the most common TAB techniques.

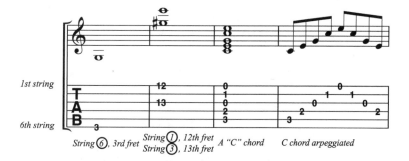

String ⑥, 3rd fret   *String ①, 12th fret*   *A "C" chord*   *C chord arpeggiated*
String ③, 13th fret

BENDING NOTES

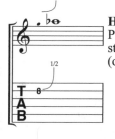

Half Step
Play the note and bend string one half step (one fret).

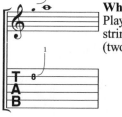

Whole Step
Play the note and bend string one whole step (two frets).

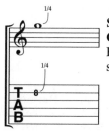

Slight Bend/ Quarter-Tone Bend
Play the note and bend string a quarter step sharp.

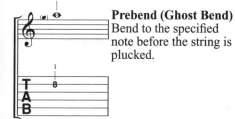

Prebend (Ghost Bend)
Bend to the specified note before the string is plucked.

Prebend and Release
Play the already-bent string, then immediately drop it down to the fretted note.

Unison Bends
Play both notes and immediately bend the lower note to the same pitch as the higher note.

Bend and Release
Play the note and bend to the next pitch, then release to the original note. Only the first note is attacked.

Bends Involving More Than One String
Play the note and bend the string while playing an additional note on another string. Upon release, relieve the pressure from the additional note allowing the original note to sound alone.

Bends Involving Stationary Notes
Play both notes and immediately bend the lower note up to pitch. Return as indicated.

ARTICULATIONS

Hammer-On
Play the lower note, then "hammer" your finger to the higher note. Only the first note is plucked.

Pull-Off
Play the higher note with your first finger already in position on the lower note. Pull your finger off the first note with a strong downward motion that plucks the string—sounding the lower note.

Legato Slide
Play the first note and, keeping pressure applied on the string, slide up to the second note.

The diagonal line shows that it is a slide and not a hammer-on or a pull-off.

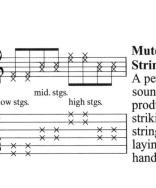
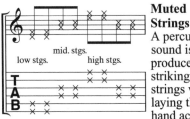

Muted Strings
A percussive sound is produced by striking the strings while laying the fretting hand across them.

Palm Mute
The notes are muted (muffled) by placing the palm of the picking hand lightly on the strings, just in front of the bridge.

HARMONICS

Natural Harmonic
A finger of the fretting hand lightly touches the string at the note indicated in the TAB and is plucked by the pick, producing a bell-like sound called a harmonic.

Artificial Harmonic
Fret the note at the first TAB number, lightly touch the string at the fret indicated in parens (usually 12 frets higher than the fretted note), then pluck the string with an available finger or your pick.

TREMOLO BAR

Specified Interval
The pitch of a note or chord is lowered to the specified interval and then returned as indicated. The action of the tremolo bar is graphically represented by the peaks and valleys of the diagram.

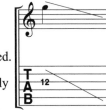

Unspecified Interval
The pitch of a note or chord is lowered, usually very dramatically, until the pitch of the string becomes indeterminate.

PICK DIRECTION

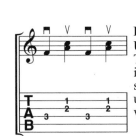

Downstrokes and Upstrokes
The downstroke is indicated with this symbol (⊓) and the upstroke is indicated with this (V).

REPEAT SIGNS

Double dots on the inside of a double bar line mean to go back to the beginning or a forward-facing repeat sign and play the same music again.

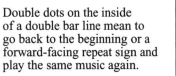

Blues Rhythm Guitar

Introduction to Blues Rhythm Guitar

Rhythm guitar is the heart and soul of blues music and should be an essential part of every guitarist's repertoire. In this section, you will learn several rhythmic variations on some of the most popular blues styles. These styles include:

- Medium blues shuffle (in the style of Stevie Ray Vaughan)
- Straight eighth blues (in the style of Chuck Berry)
- Blues-rock shuffle (in the style of Eric Clapton)
- Uptown/jump blues (in the style of B. B. King)
- Slow blues (in the style of Jimi Hendrix)
- Mambo blues (in the style of Albert King)

This section explores many different examples for each of the six blues styles above. The examples increase progressively in difficulty from fairly simple to challenging—both rhythmically and harmonically. Each blues style incorporates typical and popular chords that best enhance the presented styles. For example, the uptown/jump blues would sound best with fuller and more complex chords than those used in a three-chord medium blues shuffle. Each style features different keys and a wide range of tempos, which makes this book a challenging and exciting practice tool.

Medium Shuffle

The *medium shuffle*, also known as medium blues shuffle, is by far the most common blues feel. Variations of it can be heard on virtually every blues album ever recorded! The medium shuffle has a forward-propelling, loping feel—check out "Pride and Joy" by Stevie Ray Vaughan for an example.

The examples in this chapter are in the key of E and range from fairly simple to progressively more challenging.

Example 1: Guitar Boogie Shuffle

This is a basic boogie blues rhythm. Strive for accuracy and mute the bass notes using the heel of your picking hand. In the example below, the tempo is shown as one quarter note equaling 100; this is a way to indicate that the tempo is 100 BPM, or beats per minute. Set your metronome to this tempo to play along with the example.

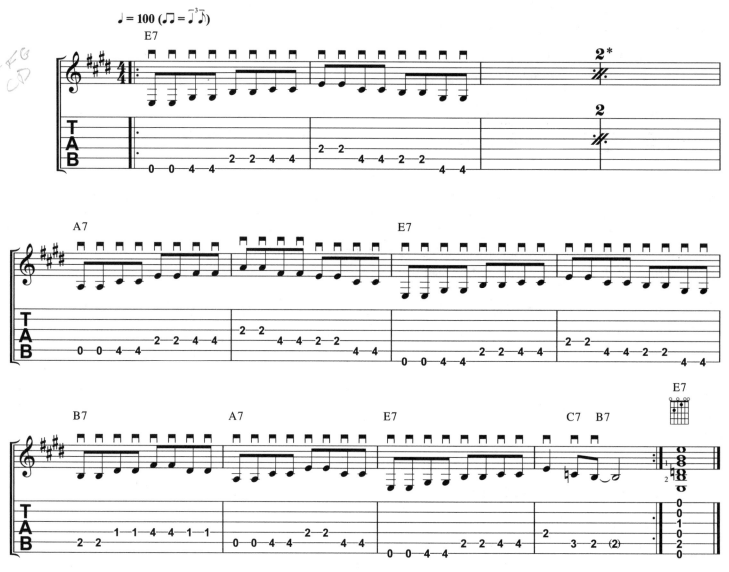

Ways to Make This Example Sound Great

- Play using only downstrokes
- Mute the bass strings near the bridge
- Maintain the "loping" feel of the shuffle throughout
- Turn up the bass on your amp to help thicken the sound
- Play using a clean guitar sound and the neck pickup

* The symbol 𝄎 means to repeat the previous two measures.

Example 2: The Zipper

Here is a variation on the basic boogie. We'll add a *chromatic* (movement in half steps) note to each figure. As in example 1, the turnaround is played on the 5th string, moving chromatically down to the "B" note from a half step above.

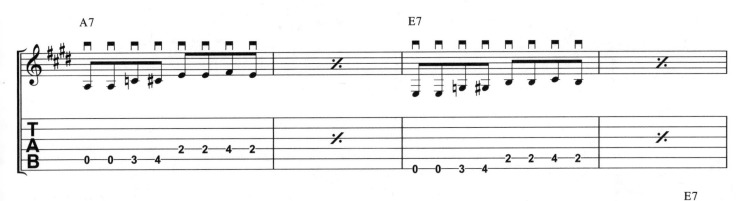

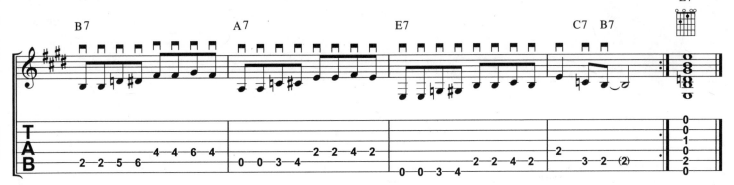

Ways to Make This Example Sound Great

- Play using only downstrokes
- Mute the bass strings using the heel of your right hand
- Crank the bass on your amp higher than you normally would

The symbol ⅊. means to repeat the previous measure.

Example 3: Memphis Fat

Here is an extremely common and popular rhythm that sounds great when doubled by the bass. The turnaround is played by sliding into the B7 chord from a half step above.

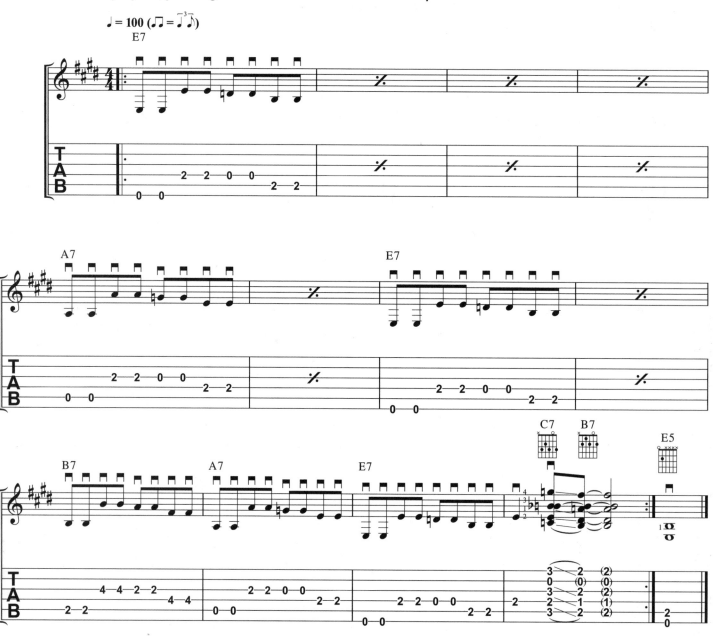

Ways to Make This Example Sound Great

- Play each note *staccato*—short, detached notes accomplished by releasing pressure on the fretted note just after it is played
- Mute the notes at the bridge using the heel of your picking hand
- Play using only downstrokes

Example 4: Dazzled

This one is reminiscent of "Dazed and Confused" by Led Zeppelin and sounds great when it is doubled by the bass player. Because only quarter notes are used, the shuffle rhythm is not actually played until the last measure, but it is implied throughout. The turnaround is played by sliding into the B7 chord from a half step above.

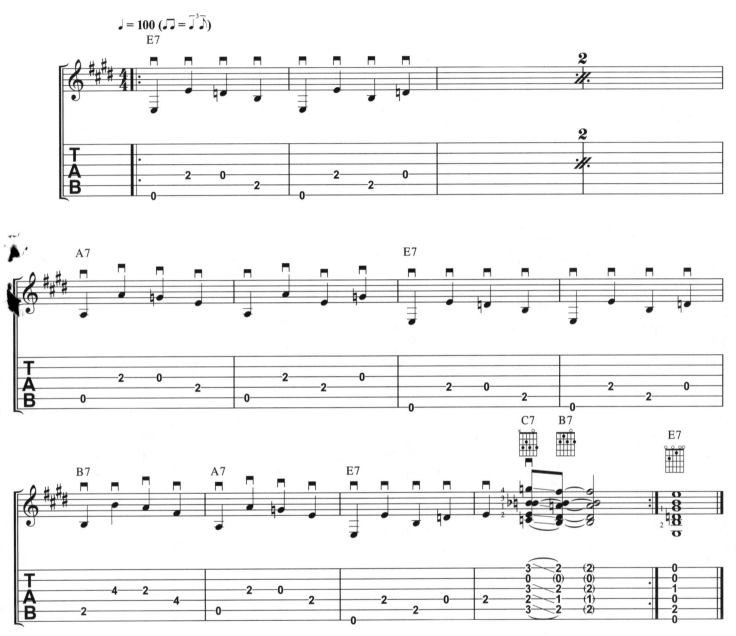

Ways to Make This Example Sound Great

- Sustain each note for its full value
- Use the bridge pickup
- Play with distortion and loudly with a rock attitude
- Use only downstrokes

Example 5: The Big One

Here is an example of one of the most basic and essential blues rhythms. It should be played in the lowest register possible for any given key. Pay attention to the fingering (indicated with small numbers next to the noteheads). In measure 9, there is a stretch with the pinky that can be challenging at first. Practice it until you feel comfortable.

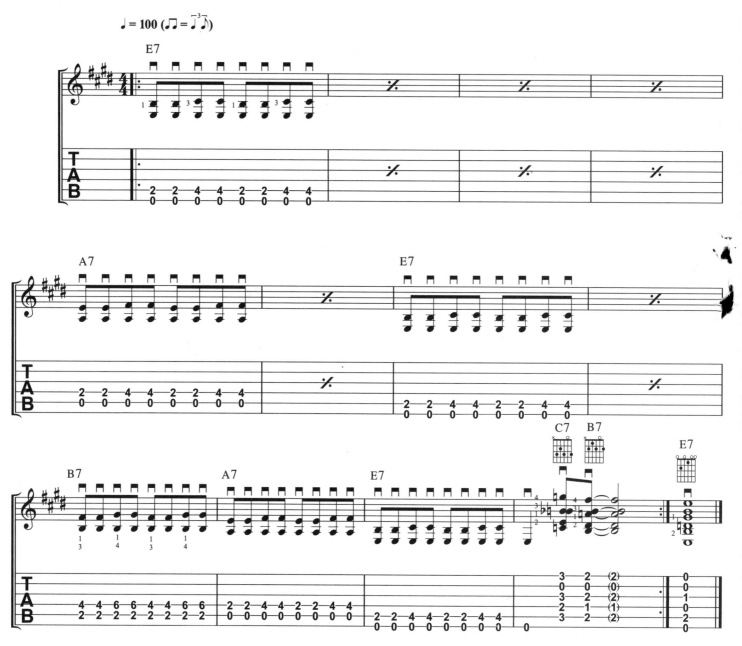

Ways to Make This Example Sound Great

- Play in the lowest register possible
- Use only downstrokes
- Palm mute the strings at the bridge
- Play with a crunch sound, in the style of Keith Richards of The Rolling Stones

---

Example 6: Slippery

This classic guitar rhythm is essential for any blues player. Notice that the example begins on beat 2 of each measure. To ensure accuracy with the timing, keep your right hand moving to the pulse of the music. When playing the slide for the A, or IV, chord, be sure to keep your fingers together so that the chord shape remains intact. The turnaround is played by sliding into the B9 chord from a half step above.

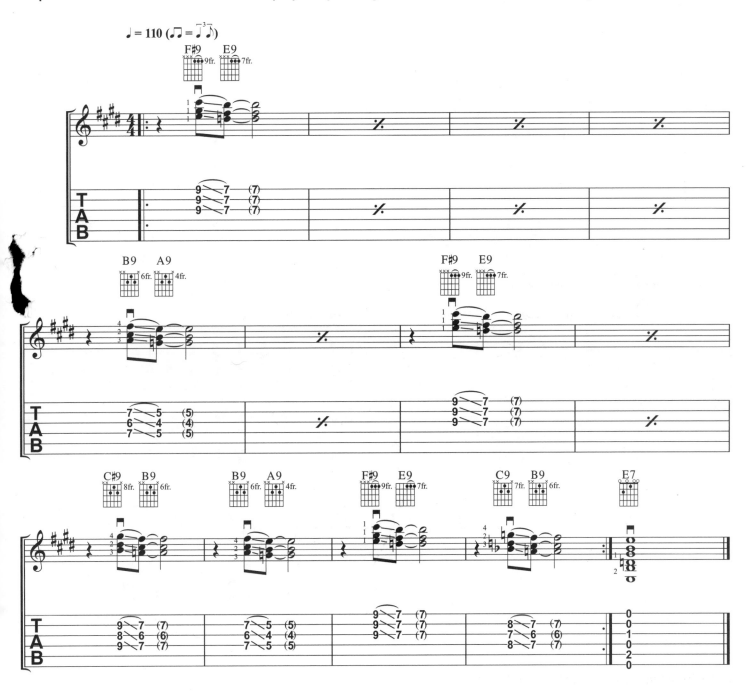

Ways to Make This Example Sound Great

- Play with a relaxed feel
- Use a clean tone on the middle or bridge pickup
- Play using only downstrokes

Example 7: The Big Bottom

This example focuses on strumming chords. The chords are played in a low register across all the strings, which produces a "big" sound. Be sure to keep your picking hand moving in time with the pulse of the music. Watch and listen to the video performance closely so you don't miss the occasional ghost-note strums—these are created by momentarily loosening your grip on the chord while continuing to strum the rhythm. The turnaround is played by sliding into the B7 chord from a half step above.

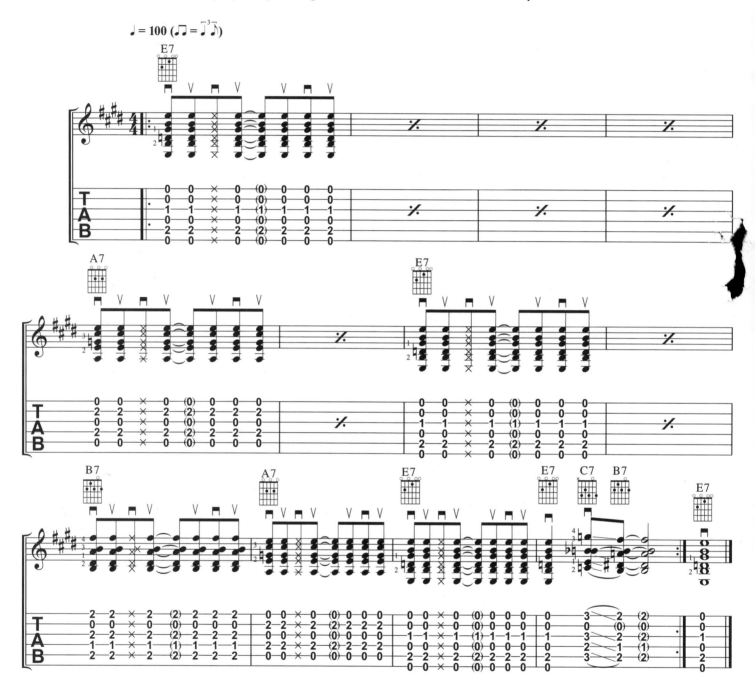

Ways to Make This Example Sound Great

- Play from the wrist and not the forearm
- Play on an acoustic guitar
- Use a very relaxed strum
- Mute all the unwanted strings with the left or fretting hand

Example 8: Icy Road

This one sounds great but is a little tricky. Since it requires many *double-stop* slides, it's important to keep your fingers together. (Double stops are simply two notes played simultaneously.) Don't leave a finger behind when you make the slide. Notice that the example begins on beat 2.

Ways to Make This Example Sound Great

- Don't grip the fretted notes too tightly—this will help keep a steady rhythm
- Keep your right hand moving in time to the pulse of the rhythm, helping to ensure accurate timing
- Don't allow your fingers to pull apart during the slides
- Use the middle or bridge pickup

Example 9: The Odd Couple

This example uses two-note chords, or *dyads.* These dyads are partial chords. Practice shifting to the IV and V chords as they both require quite a jump on the fretboard.

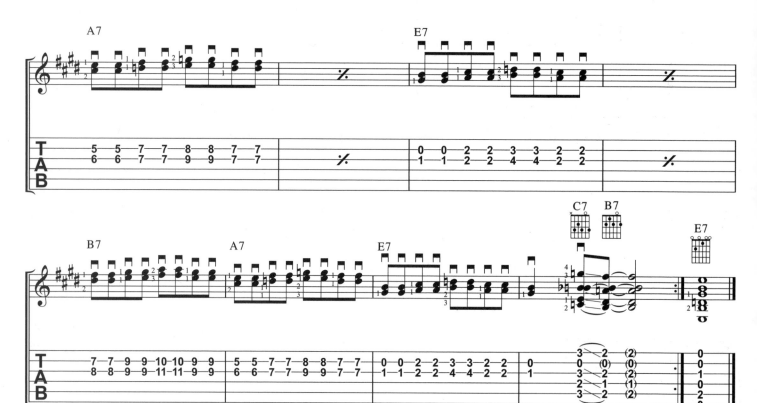

Ways to Make This Example Sound Great

- Use a clean or slightly overdriven sound
- Play using only downstrokes
- Strictly maintain the shuffle feel throughout

Example 10: The Rumble

This example has a raw bluesy attitude and sounds a little *dissonant*, or tense sounding. Strum each chord while keeping your hand moving in time to the pulse of the music. On beats 2 and 4 of each measure, you are going to add a dissonant note.

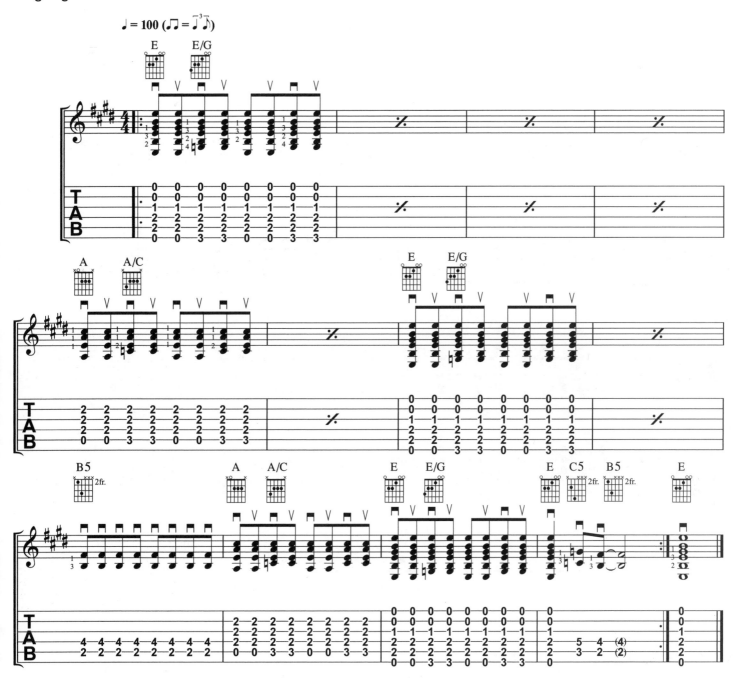

Ways to Make This Example Sound Great

- Keep your right hand moving in time to the pulse of the music, maintaining the shuffle feel
- Play loosely from your wrist and not with your forearm
- Play it as nasty as you can with distortion and attitude

Example 11: Austin's Pride

Here it is! The "daddy" of all Stevie Ray Vaughan rhythms. His classic "Pride and Joy" has become a blues anthem and some version of it should be played as part of everyone's arsenal of blues rhythms. This example simplifies the original version while maintaining the sound and attitude.

This is perhaps the trickiest rhythm in this chapter because of the right-hand movement. You are going to play only bass notes on the downstrokes and only open strings on the upstroke. You'll need to mute the unwanted strings on the downstrokes using fingers on your fretting hand. A slightly circular picking motion helps keep it feeling relaxed.

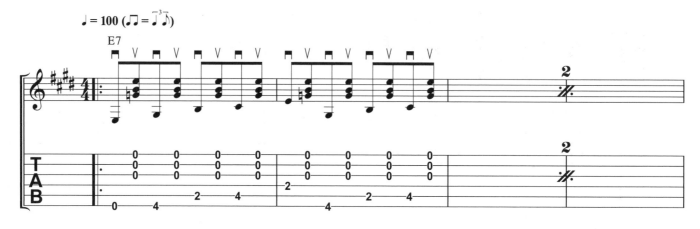

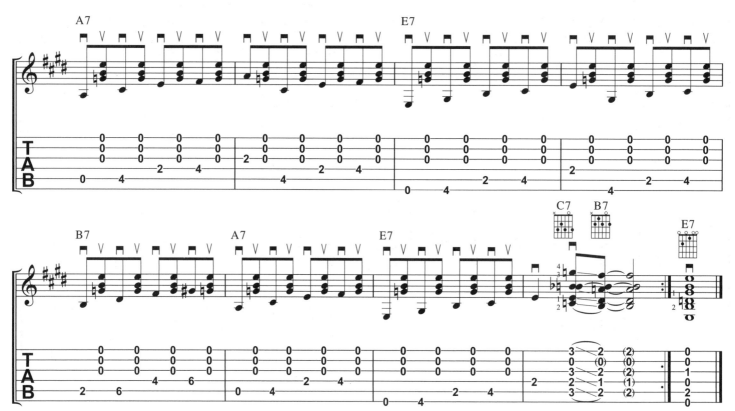

Ways to Make This Example Sound Great

- Play using your forearm for overall power
- Use a circular motion with your picking hand
- Mute all unwanted strings on the downstrokes and play only the bass note
- Crank up the overdrive and let 'er rip

Example 12: The Back Stack

This one is great because you join the other players in the rhythm section of the band by doubling the drummer's snare drum. Keep your right hand moving in time to the pulse of the music. "Float" your picking hand slightly over the strings, ghosting the downstrokes, and play the chord aggressively on the upstrokes.

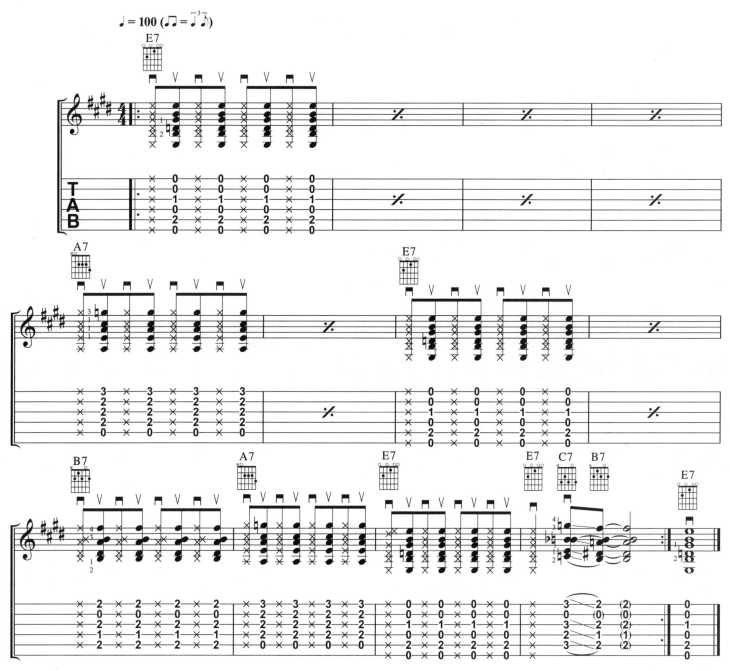

Ways to Make This Example Sound Great

- Strum using your forearm for power
- Keep your right hand moving in time to the pulse of the music
- Grab the strings and mute them all using your left hand so that they are staccato

Straight Eighths

Another popular groove for the blues is the *straight eighths,* or straight eighth-note, feel. This feel is generally found in blues-rock or rhythm & blues, with "Mary Had a Little Lamb" by Stevie Ray Vaughan being a great example of straight eighth-note blues-rock. You'll also find this feel in classic songs by Gary Moore, Wilson Pickett, The Butterfield Blues Band, Creedence Clearwater Revival, ZZ Top, and more. The basic feel is set up by the drummer playing a basic rock beat, with the snare drum on beats 2 and 4. The bass player and guitarist then double the single-note rhythm. The guitar will usually play in the lowest register possible.

All the examples in this chapter are in the key of C, except Examples 1 and 8, which are in the key of E. The examples range from fairly simple to progressively more challenging. Each example, however, contains within it an objective and is designed to demonstrate a specific aspect of blues guitar rhythm.

Example 1: On the Lamb

This example is in the style of "Mary Had a Little Lamb" by Stevie Ray Vaughan. It is a call and response type rhythm. The guitar will play a single-note rhythm and then answer it with chords.

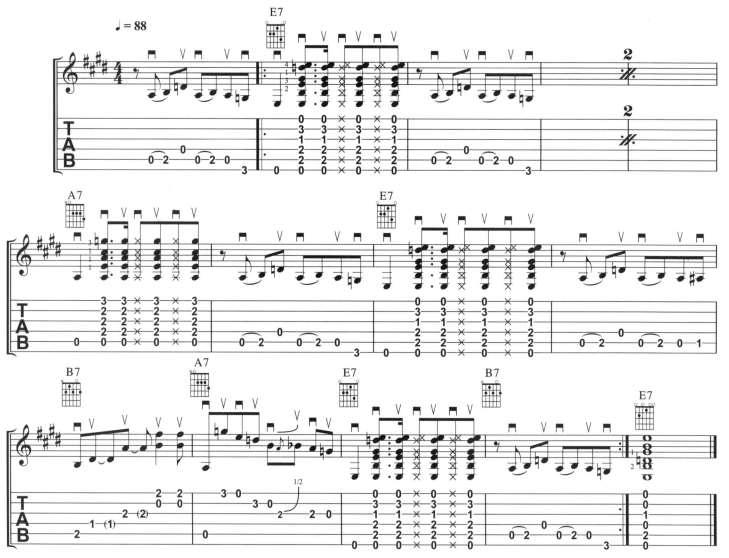

Ways to Make This Example Sound Great

- Use all downstrokes for the single notes
- Use a clean sound and add a bit of reverb
- Use your neck pickup to create a "boomy" sound

Example 2: Lord Mr. Ford

Here is a cool rhythm that works well for a classic R&B sound or a nasty ZZ Top sound.

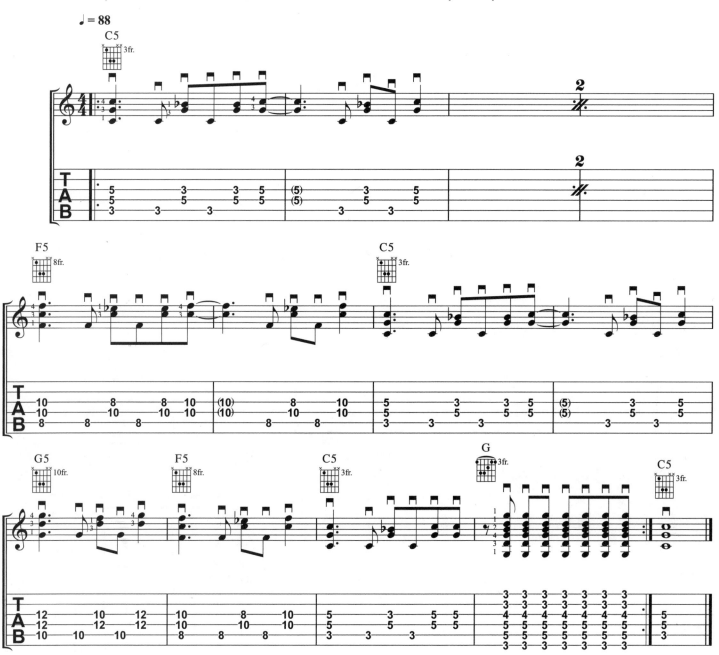

Ways to Make This Example Sound Great

- Keep your fretting fingers arched over the fretboard so that all the strings played continue to ring
- Play with all downstrokes
- Use either a clean sound or a crunchy overdriven sound with the neck pickup

Example 3: Short & Sweet

This is an essential rhythm for every blues guitarist. Play a short staccato chord on beats 2 and 4.

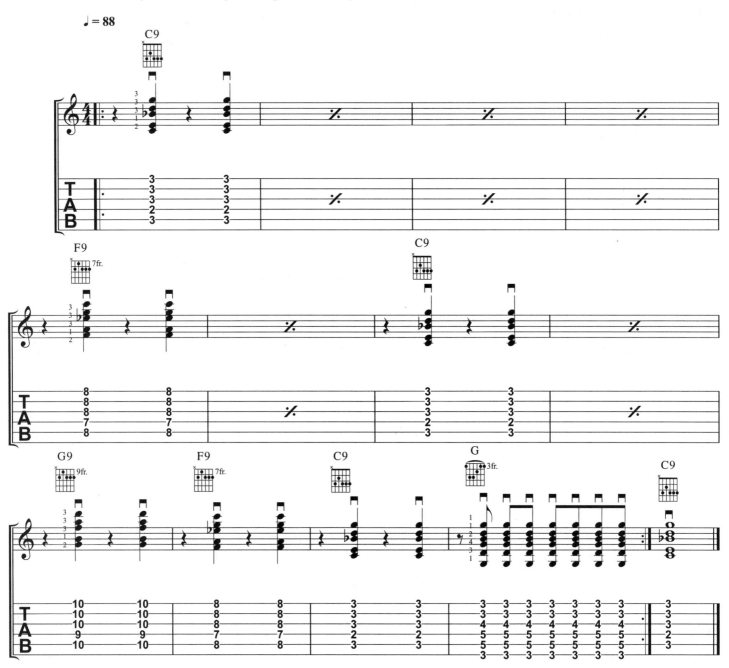

Ways to Make This Example Sound Great

- Play using a clean sound with a bit of reverb
- Play the chords staccato
- Loosen your grip on the chords after you pick them to stop the ringing and create a tight, short attack
- Use your middle or neck pickup

Example 4: The New Shoes Blues

This one is like playing two parts at the same time! It features single notes and a chord "stab" on beat 2. The bass guitar part would double the single-note part.

Ways to Make This Example Sound Great

- Use a clean or slightly overdriven tone
- Allow both the single notes and the chords to ring as long as possible
- Snap your wrist when you play the chord to be sure the rhythm is accurate and tight
- Have the bass player double the single notes but not the chords

Example 5: Too Tall Holmes

This rhythm features a chromatic single-note line popular in Detroit-style blues. It has a distinct rhythm & blues sound and works best when it is doubled by the bass guitar.

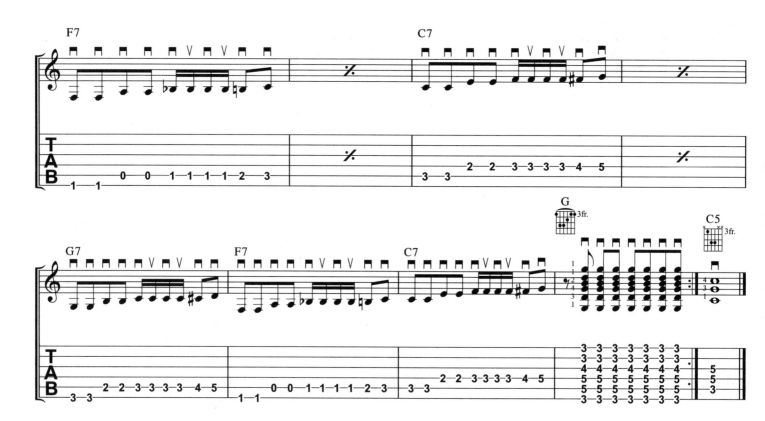

Ways to Make This Example Sound Great

- Slightly mute the notes with the palm of your fretting hand
- Dial in a stinging clean sound with lots of treble
- Don't add any reverb
- Use your bridge pickup for twang

Example 6: Filthy McNasty

The essence of this example is the octave jump, which is repeated throughout.

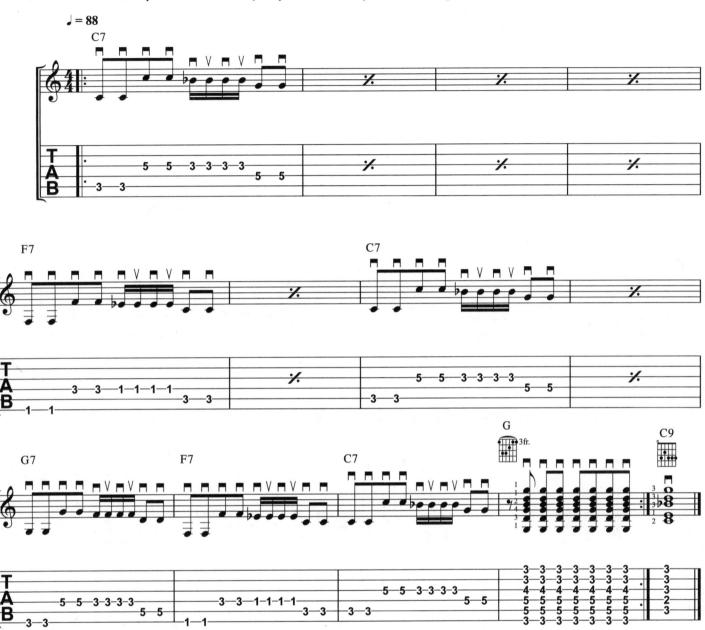

Ways to Make This Example Sound Great

- Use a heavy distortion sound
- Play in the lowest register possible
- Have the bass player double your part
- Play with a nasty rock attitude

Example 7: Book on Outta Here

This example is something blues rhythm guitar master Steve Cropper might have played during a recording session with R&B legends Booker T. & the M.G.'s. The double stops are very syncopated, so watch and listen carefully to the demonstration on the video. Imitate the exact rhythm, as it grooves and has a funky R&B twist.

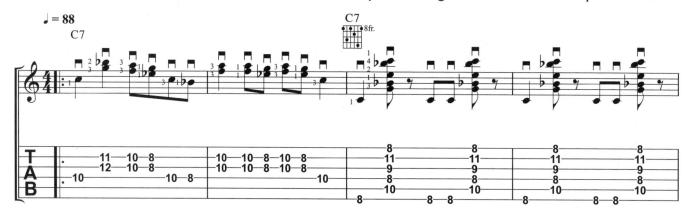

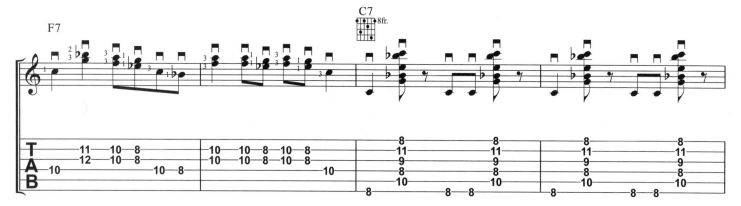

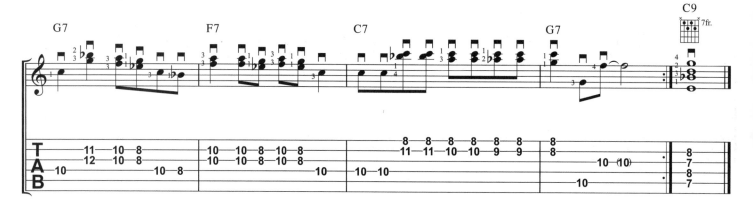

Ways to Make This Example Sound Great

- Strike the strings lightly and don't pick too hard
- Play with finesse
- Strum as close to the fretboard as you can to create a warm, round sound

Example 8: Johnny Clear

The following is in the style of John Fogerty from Creedence Clearwater Revival. This simple but essential rhythm is a must for every blues guitarist. The smaller notehead, which first appears on beat 3 of measure 1, is called a *grace note*—a quick note played before the beat.

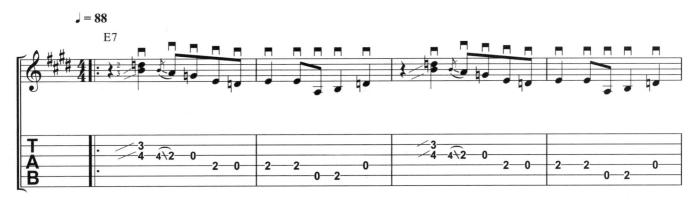

Ways to Make This Example Sound Great

- Use a clean to slightly overdriven sound
- Play the single notes precisely as written
- Play the example staccato

Example 9: Sticky Figs

This is a versatile rhythm that may be played in a funky R&B style or cranked up for a driving blues-rock style. It can be heard in songs by artists ranging from Otis Redding to Stevie Ray Vaughan.

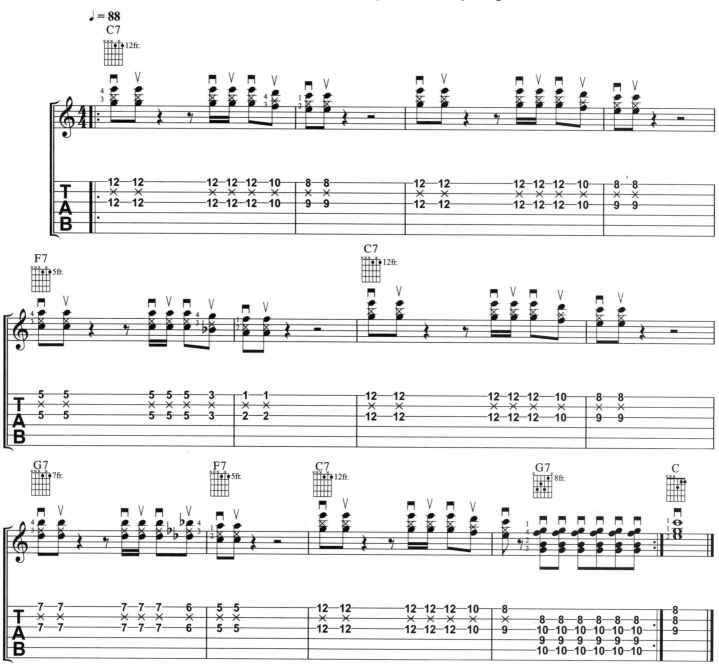

Ways to Make This Example Sound Great

- Use a clean tone for an R&B sound
- Use an overdriven tone for a rock sound
- Keep your right hand moving in time to the pulse of the music

Example 10: Your Feet's Too Big

Here is a swampy-sounding rhythm in the style of the great New Orleans band Little Feat. The overall sound is funky but with roots in the blues. Check it out.

Ways to Make This Example Sound Great

- Dial in a smooth overdrive tone
- Have the bass player double the part
- Play the first note of each phrase staccato

Example 11: Jazz Bow

If this one sounds familiar it is because it's in the style of the popular song "Sharp Dressed Man" by ZZ Top, a blues-rock classic. This one features double stops and an overdriven "jacked up" tone to give it a cool rock sound.

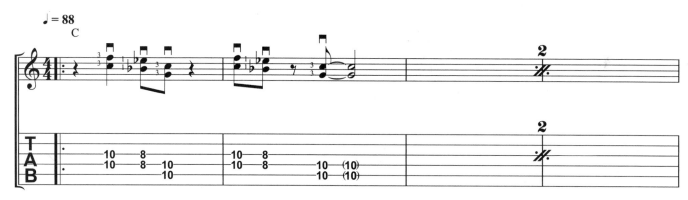

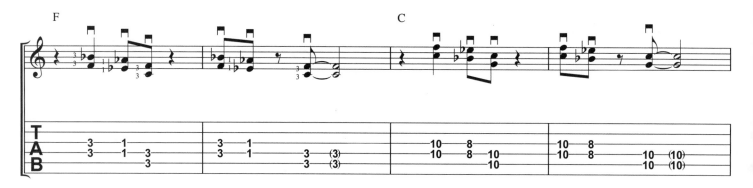

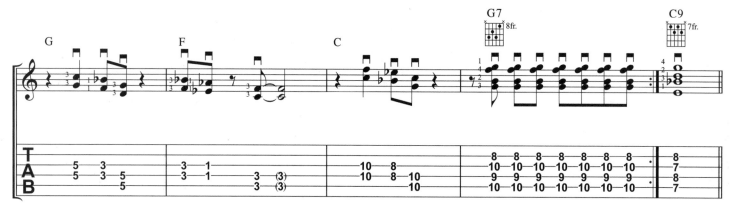

Ways to Make This Example Sound Great

- Dial in a heavy distorted tone
- Play it heavy handed
- Use the neck pickup
- Use humbucking pickups

Example 12: Pay the Man

This one is the granddaddy of all blues rhythms and has been used more often than any other blues rhythm.

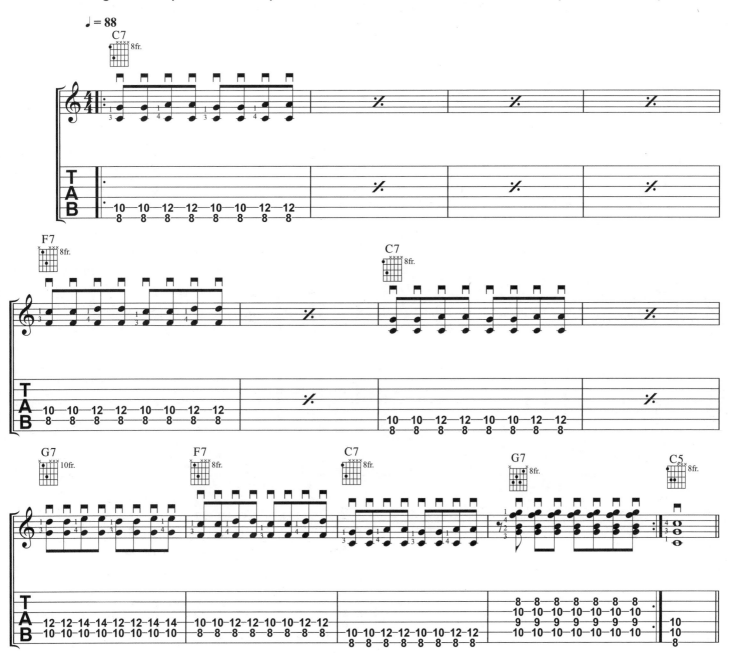

Ways to Make This Example Sound Great

- Dial in a clean or slightly overdriven sound
- Mute the bass notes with the palm of your picking hand
- Use your neck pickup
- Play with all downstrokes

Blues-Rock Shuffle

In this chapter, you'll learn how to play the *blues-rock shuffle* rhythm. The key element to this style is to use overdrive and distortion to create a blues with an attitude. Artists who commonly play in this style include Johnny Winter, John Mayer, George Thorogood, Eric Clapton, Eddie Van Halen, Gary Moore, and Ted Nugent.

The examples in this chapter are in the key of A and range from fairly simple to progressively more challenging.

Example 1: Blues for Breakfast

This example is certainly an essential blues-rock rhythm. It should be played using nasty overdrive or distortion. Play the rhythm with no palm muting, and let the strings ring out. It should sound a bit sloppy. This is what gives it attitude. Notice the single-note turnaround in measures 11–12.

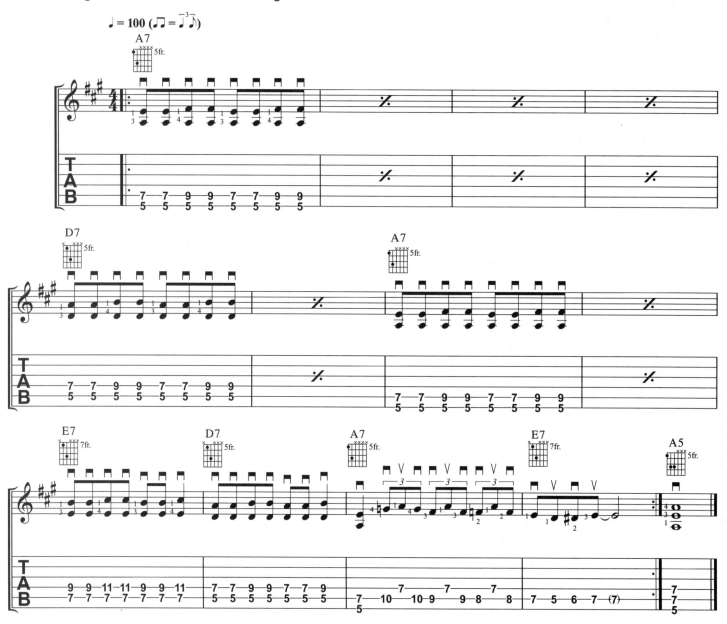

Ways to Make This Example Sound Great

- Dial in a distorted rock tone on your amp and use the bridge pickup
- Allow all the strings to ring rather than using a palm mute
- Strum from the wrist and not the arm
- Dig in and pick hard

Example 2: Revellator

This one alternates between two chords. It is a moveable riff and may be played in any key. This one also includes a single-note turnaround; it is played by alternating between the 3rd and 1st strings.

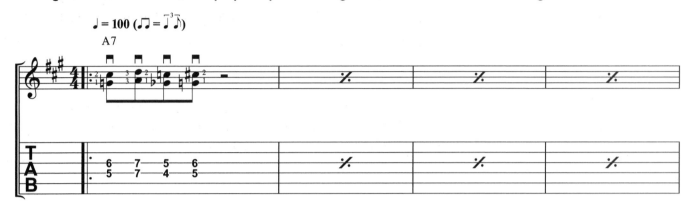

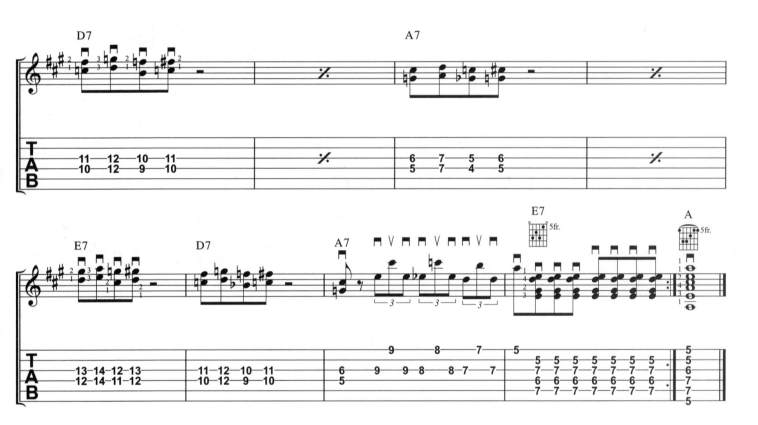

Ways to Make This Example Sound Great

- Play all the chord shapes on strings 3 and 4—while muting the remaining strings with your fretting hand
- Continue to strum along with the pulse of the music, ensuring an accurate time feel
- Play with an overdriven tone, though be careful, as too much overdrive or distortion tends to muddy the chords

Example 3: Mission Ten Eleven

The riff in this example alternates between two chords, the first of which is a minor chord. Playing a minor chord over a major progression is very common and helps imply the blues sound.

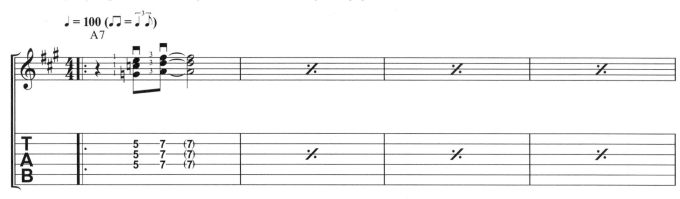

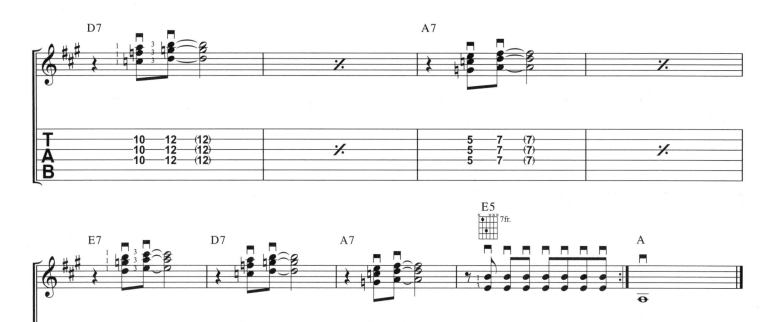

Ways to Make This Example Sound Great

- Dial in a warm, crunchy tone, but, remember, too much distortion can muddy the notes
- Continue to strum in time to the pulse of the music
- Play only strings 2, 3, and 4—with a controlled strum that will help you avoid playing unwanted strings
- Play the first chord staccato while sustaining the second chord

Example 4: Clearly a Habit

The following is another well-worn rhythm style. It features a two-bar phrase, with double stops beginning on beat 2 of the first bar. Let each chord ring for an entire beat, though it can be a bit tricky because you will need to shift positions. Master this before playing up to tempo. Notice how the pattern changes during measures 9–12.

Ways to Make This Example Sound Great

- Play in a relaxed, lazy way
- Dial in a fairly clean sound or add a chorus effect with the depth and rate knobs turned up all the way—the sound will simulate that of a Hammond organ
- Play only strings 2 and 3, but be sure to mute the unwanted strings to prevent extraneous noise

Example 5: Slidin' Around

This one is a variation of a common blues idea. Play a chord and then slide up a whole step; don't let your fingers separate as you slide. Use your 1st finger for the slide in measures 5, 6, 9, and 10. This rhythm is in the spirit of blues greats Buddy Guy, Michael Bloomfield, and Stevie Ray Vaughan.

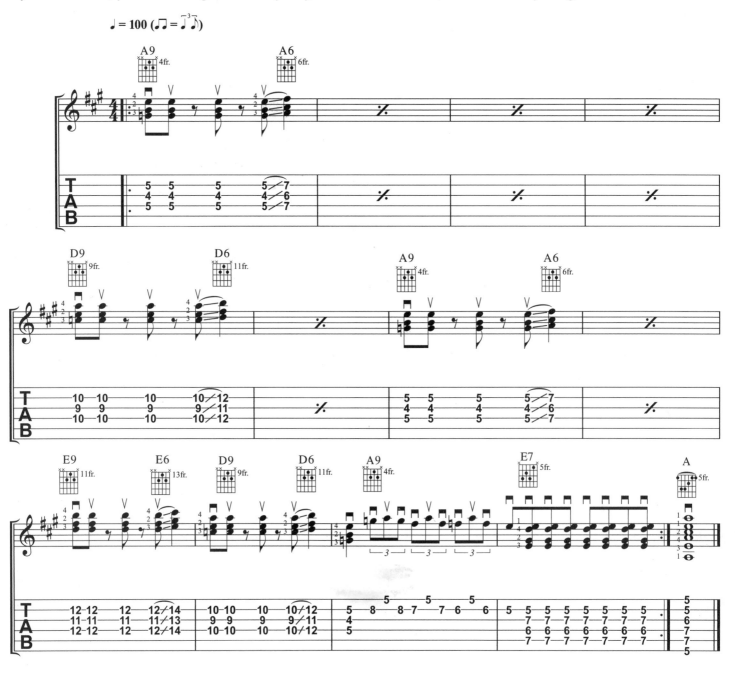

Ways to Make This Example Sound Great

- Don't allow your fingers to come apart from the shape as you move across the fretboard, and be sure to apply consistent pressure on the strings as you slide
- Keep your right hand moving in time to the pulse of the music
- Loosen your grip on the chords to mute the strings during rests
- Play the single-note turnaround on strings 1 and 2, though keep the high note fixed while the lower note descends in half steps

Example 6: The Main Squeeze

This single-note rhythm works great in a blues-rock setting. The quarter notes give it a driving feel. Keep the time steady and allow each note to ring. An aggressive right hand will bring this progression to life. The turnaround is played primarily on strings 6 and 5.

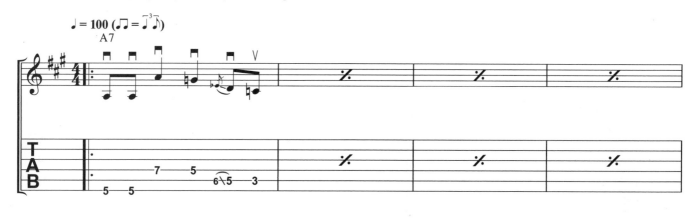

Ways to Make This Example Sound Great

- Use a hard-driving rock distortion tone
- Allow each note to ring for the duration of a quarter note
- Play the slides as a grace note and with no time value
- Mute the unwanted strings using the palm of your picking hand

Example 7: Green and Blues

Power chords, which consist of the 1st and 5th degrees of the major scale, add a rock edge to any song. This example is reminiscent of "Green Onions" by Booker T. & the M.G.'s. A rock sound can be applied here through the addition of an overdriven tone. The slower tempo adds heaviness to it. Mute unwanted strings using the palm of your picking hand.

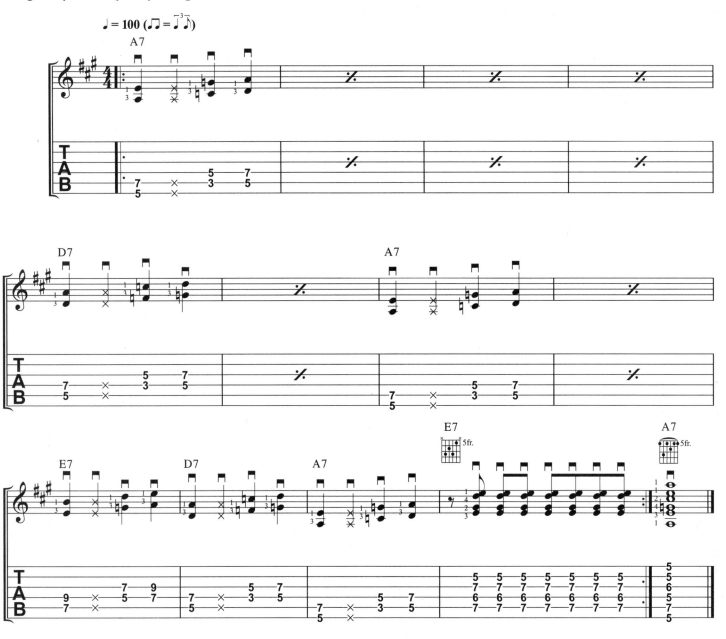

Ways to Make This Example Sound Great

- Play using a heavy overdrive or distortion sound
- Have the bass guitar double you if you are playing with a band
- Use the bridge pickup
- Hold the chords for their entire duration

Example 8: Due Props

This one combines single notes with double stops. The single-note riff is played and then followed by the double stops to create a call and response effect. Notice the rhythm doesn't change when the chords change. Using one phrase through an entire progression sounds great and is often neglected. Play and repeat the phrase over all of the chords in the progression. The slide in measure 2 does not have an actual time value and should be played as a grace note. Use your 1st and 3rd fingers for the double stops, and allow the last double stop of the phrase to ring for its entire value.

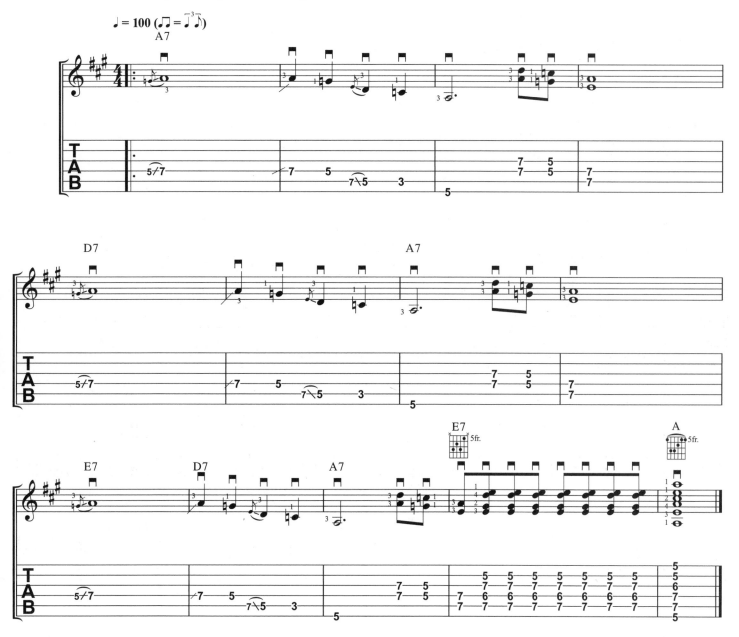

Ways to Make This Example Sound Great

- Play using a silky, smooth sustaining overdrive tone
- Add a bit of vibrato to the first and last notes of the single-note phrase
- Play the double stops using downstrokes
- Play the slide on string 5 with your 3rd finger

Example 9: Zample Pample

This is a classic must-know blues-rock rhythm reminiscent of Gary Moore or ZZ Top. It's played in the open position and combines single notes and power chords. Add a slight bend to the fretted single notes. The turnaround at the end is played using descending single notes on the 5th and 6th strings.

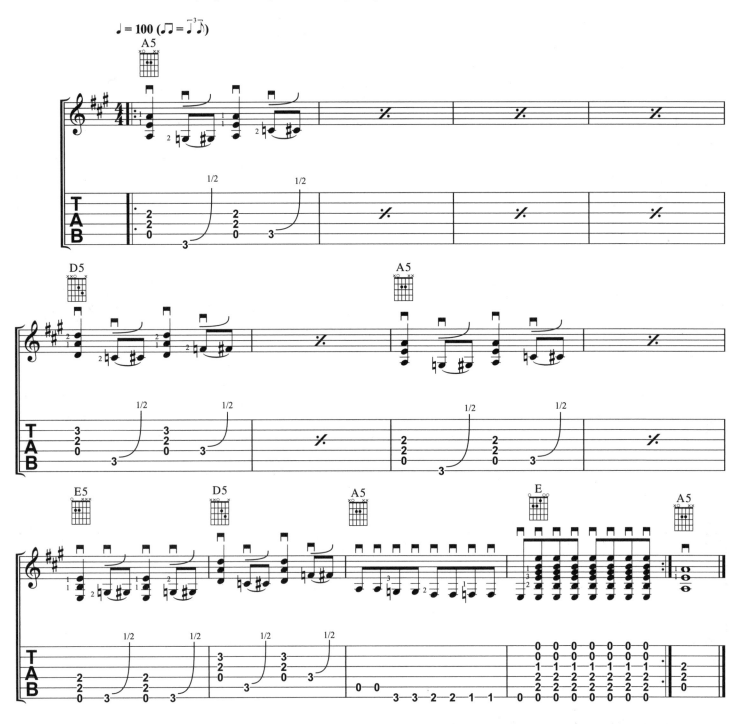

Ways to Make This Example Sound Great

- Play with a nasty distortion
- Add a slight bend to each of the fretted single notes
- Play using all downstrokes
- Keep the tempo of the rhythm steady and even
- Have the bass player double the rhythm if you are playing in a band

Example 10: Rough Neck

The use of single notes, chromatic notes, and double stops keeps this rhythm interesting and unpredictable. Play it in the 5th position. The octaves are played on strings 6 and 4 respectively. The double stops are played on strings 5 and 4. The turnaround is played using power chords.

Ways to Make This Example Sound Great

- Play with a distorted heavy-rock tone
- Keep the time steady and even
- Have the bass player double the rhythm if you are playing this in a band
- Make sure you don't play the unwanted strings; this will require you to have concise picking technique
- Mute all unwanted strings with the palm of your picking hand

Uptown/Jump Blues

The *uptown/jump blues* is a fairly sophisticated feel. It is usually played quite fast and is reminiscent of B. B. King's "Everyday I Have the Blues." Other artists who have popularized the feel are Brian Setzer, Big Bad Voodoo Daddy, Reverend Horton Heat, Big Sandy and His Fly-Rite Boys, Rod Piazza & the Mighty Flyers, and The Fabulous Thunderbirds. The basic feel is anchored by the drummer and bass player playing quarter notes on the downbeat. The drummer plays quarter notes on the kick drum, and the bass player will double it, playing a boogie-woogie style rhythm part.

The examples in this chapter are in the key of G and range from fairly simple to progressively more challenging.

Example 1: Back Home Blues

This is an interesting rhythm that features dyads. The rhythm is played using two eighth notes on the *backbeat* of each measure. (Backbeat means beats 2 and 4.) The first four measures outline the I chord. Move the dyad down a half step in measures 5 and 6, and this will outline the IV chord. Moving the dyad up a half step in measure 9 will outline the V7 chord.

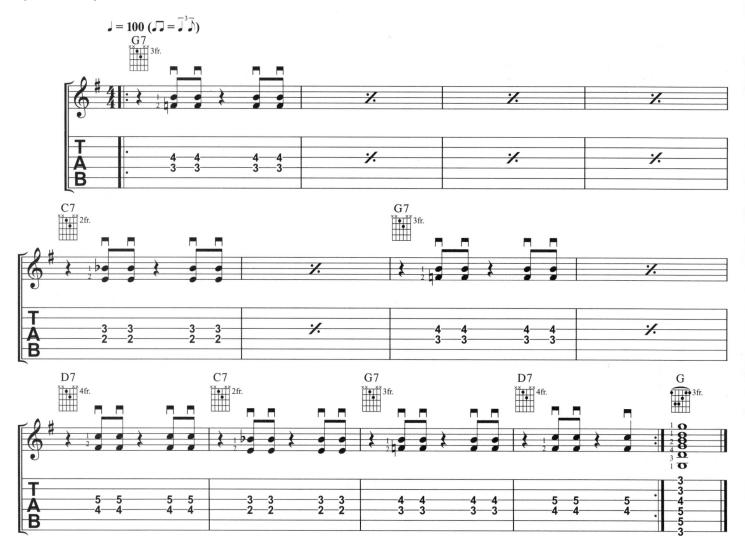

Ways to Make This Example Sound Great

- Loosen your grip between each strum to make the dyads sound staccato
- Keep your right hand moving in time to the pulse of the music to ensure a good time feel
- Employ the neck pickup for a smooth, warm tone

Example 2: Kansas City Stomp

This is an essential rhythm for the uptown/jump blues feel. This rhythm matches the backbeat of the snare drum. Keep your hand moving in time to the pulse of the music.

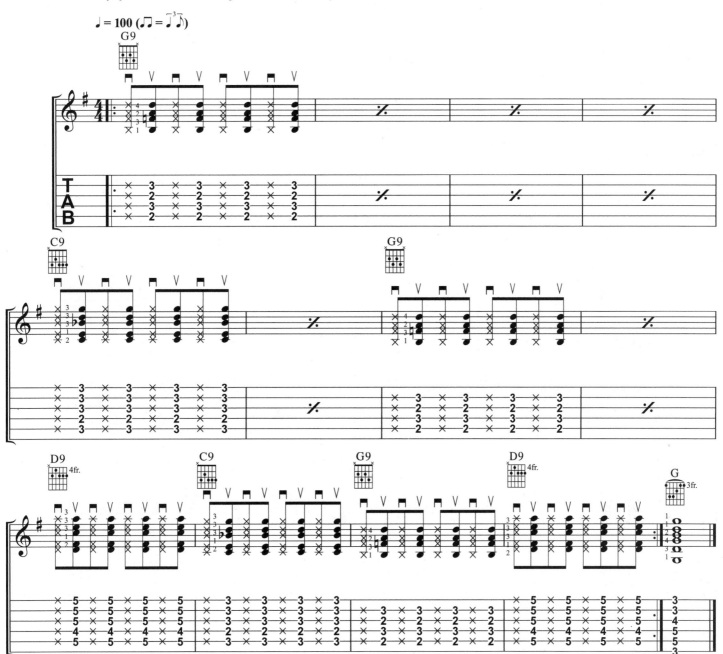

Ways to Make This Example Sound Great

- Loosen your grip between each strum to make the chords sound staccato
- Keep your right hand moving in time to the pulse of the music to ensure a good time feel
- Use the neck pickup for a smooth, warm tone

Example 3: The Turnpike

Keith Richards of The Rolling Stones played a variation of this rhythm on their cover version of the R&B hit "Route 66." Interestingly, the first double stop outlines the IV chord of the blues progression. Make sure the hammer-on is sounded clearly, as it provides movement to the sound.

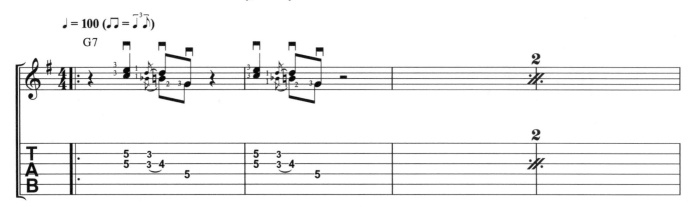

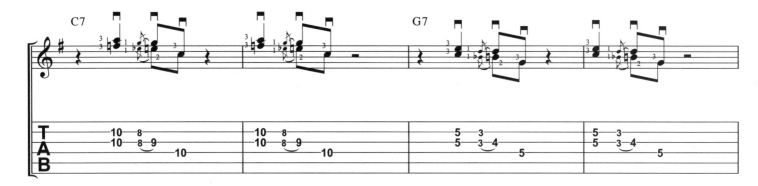

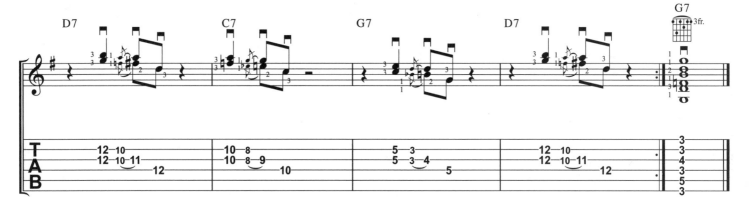

Ways to Make This Example Sound Great

- Dial in a warm, clean tone on your amp
- Be sure not to play on beat 1
- Keep your picking hand moving in time to the music
- Be sure to play the hammer-on aggressively

Example 4: Slithery

Be sure to choke each triad after you play it to maintain a staccato feel—as if you are playing a drum.

Ways to Make This Example Sound Great

- Keep your picking hand moving in time to the music, using a downstroke for the downbeats and an upstroke for the upbeats
- Loosen your grip after playing each chord so it sounds staccato
- Use your 1st finger to play the half-step slide on the 5th string

Example 5: Detroit Banger

This one features a slide into each chord from a half step below. It's a very popular blues rhythm technique and works for almost every tempo of blues. The chords are all dominant 9th chords.

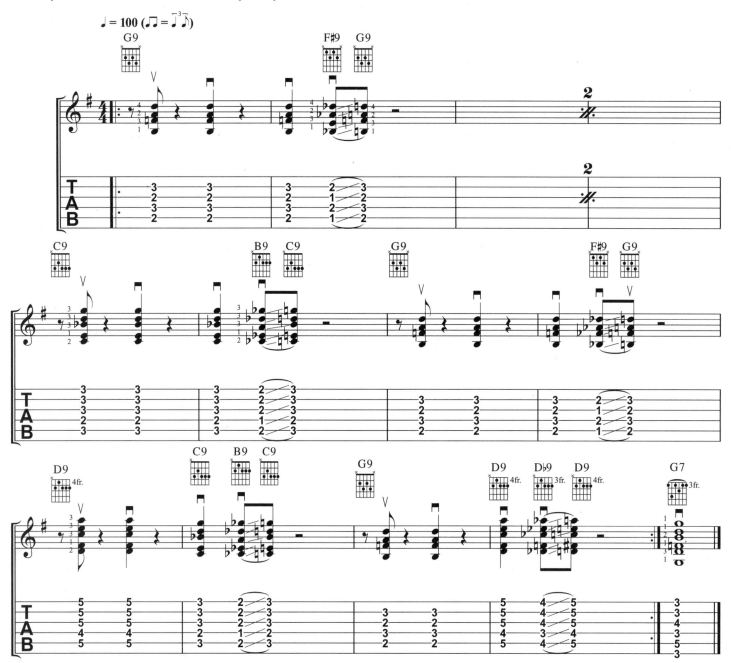

Ways to Make This Example Sound Great

- Keep steady and accurate time with both your picking and fretting hands
- Keep the chord shape intact when sliding; don't let your fingers slip apart
- During the rests, maintain the rhythm by strumming in time to the pulse of the beat

---

Example 6: Floatin' on Down to Cotton Town

Here, you'll approach each chord from a half step above. This is a common blues technique and adds movement to a progression. The chords are dominant 9th chords. Be sure to practice this in different keys!

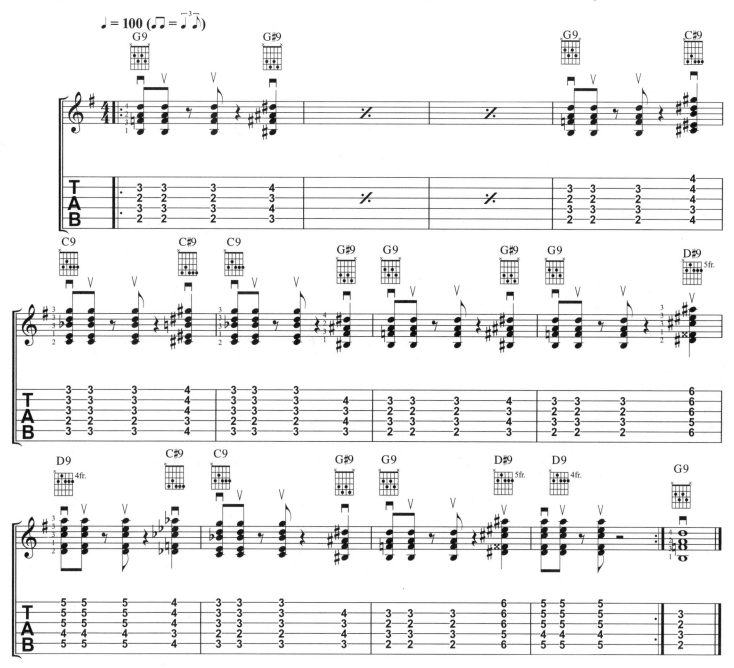

Ways to Make This Example Sound Great

- Keep steady and accurate time with both your picking and fretting hands
- Keep the chord shape intact when sliding; don't let your fingers slip apart
- Maintain pressure on the chord as you slide down so that the notes do not stop ringing
- Maintain the rhythm by strumming in time to the pulse of the beat

Example 7: Swing Street

Imagine a four-piece horn section playing together and driving B. B. King's band to a feverish pitch. The idea of the "horn punch rhythm" in this example is to simulate that effect. The dominant 9th chord voicings provide a slick, uptown sound.

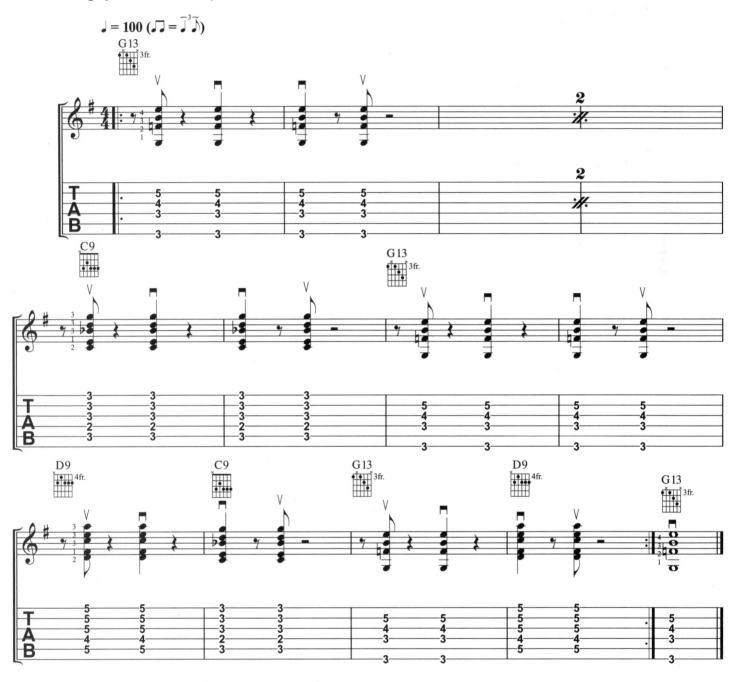

Ways to Make This Example Sound Great

- Pick using short, brassy, staccato stabs
- Use the bridge pickup
- Keep steady and accurate time with both your picking and fretting hands
- Maintain the rhythm by strumming in time to the pulse of the beat

Example 8: Hoopie Do

This is a great "in the pocket" jazzy rhythm that uses dominant 13th chords, which were also found in the previous example. The richer chord voicings, although a bit more challenging to play, create a sophisticated sound. The turnaround is played by moving the chords down in half steps. These chords can be used to replace the more common dominant 7th chord voicings at any time as long as you alert the rest of the band, so that they're not caught off guard.

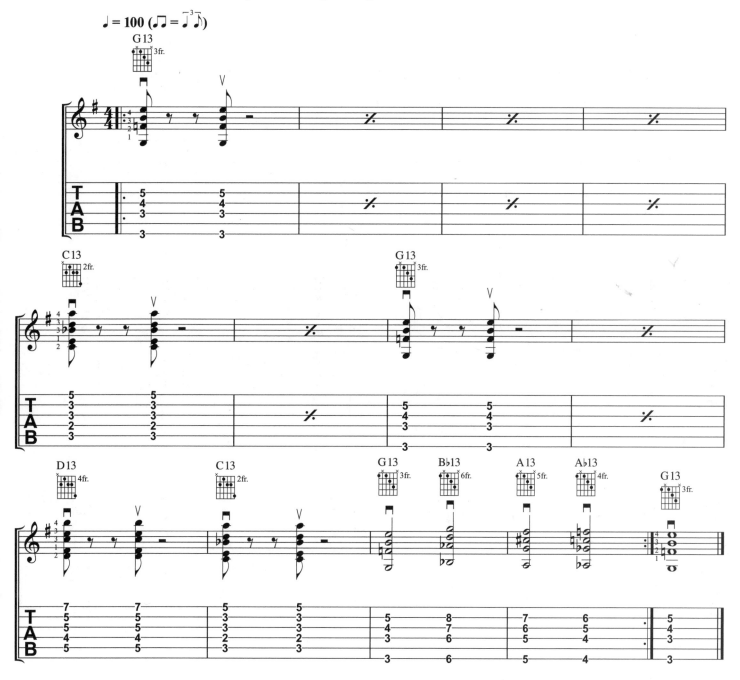

Ways to Make This Example Sound Great

- Play using staccato downstrokes
- Make the pick attack sharp and definitive
- Play using a brassy, trebly tone on the bridge pickup

Example 9: Big City Lights

This example features chords with more complex fingerings. These voicings are typical of an actual horn section. In this example, the top voice moves like a lead trumpet in a horn section. The movement is executed by pulling off with your little finger. For the C9 and D9 chords, the lower note of the pull-off is played on the 1st string using a 1st-finger barre across the top two strings. Dominant 9th and 13th chords are used throughout the entire example.

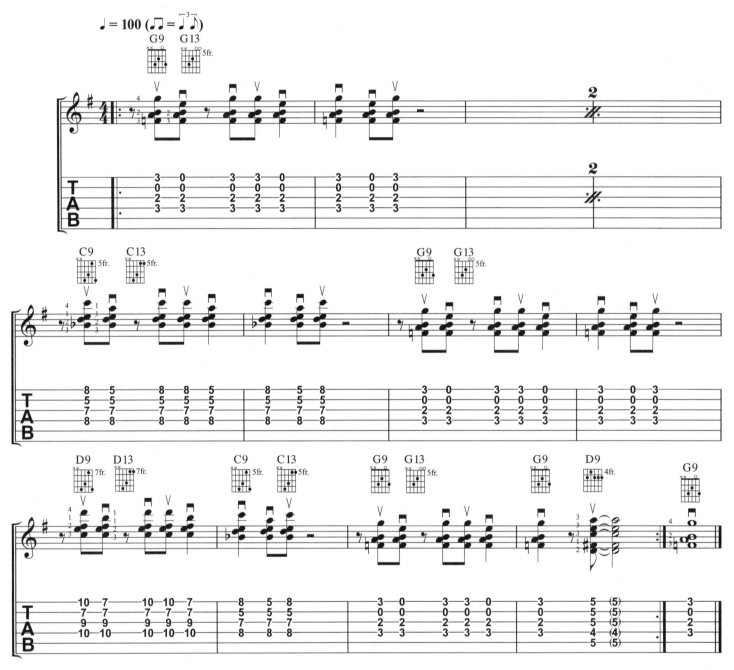

Ways to Make This Example Sound Great

- Use a sharp, percussive attack
- Dial in a clean, brassy tone
- Use the bridge pickup
- Strum only the top four strings
- Don't play the lower strings accidentally as that creates unwanted, extraneous noise—you may even be playing notes that are not in the key, creating dissonance

Slow Blues

In this chapter, you'll learn how to play variations on a *slow blues.* Slow blues is perhaps the most expressive and emotional blues feel. It can be heard on The Allman Brothers' version of "Stormy Monday Blues," "Texas Flood" by Stevie Ray Vaughan, and "Red House" by Jimi Hendrix.

The slow blues is usually played over the standard 12-bar form. Some use a *quick change,* which means the IV chord replaces the I chord in measure 2, and then goes back to the I chord in measures 3 and 4. The examples in this chapter are in the key of A, and they range from fairly simple to progressively more challenging.

Example 1: When the Levy Breaks

Here, we have perhaps the most common rhythm for the slow blues: the *chord slide.* This rhythm is well-suited for the slow blues and is essential for any blues guitarist to learn. The chord slide consists of whole-step slides on each chord. Play the first chord and then slide down to the second.

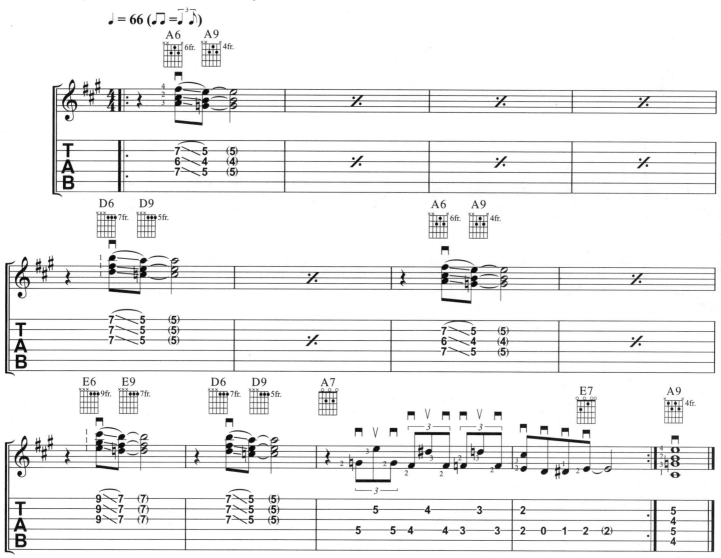

Ways to Make This Example Sound Great

- Play the chord prior to the slide using a downstroke
- Play the chord slide by moving the first chord shape down a whole step without releasing pressure on the strings—the second chord of the slide should sustain for the remainder of the measure
- Don't allow your fingers to come apart when you slide
- Use only one pick stroke per measure
- Dial in a clean or slightly overdriven tone (remember that too much distortion will muddy the chords)

Example 2: The Bump

This one is reminiscent of what a keyboardist might play. It is a subtle variation and should be played lightly or it can sound overbearing or distracting. Although it is not a quick change blues, the notes in measure 2 imply the IV chord. It is not necessary for other instruments in the band to follow; it's quite common for the guitar to imply the IV chord while the rest of the band stays with the I chord. Measure 11 has an interesting three-note chord turnaround that should be added to your arsenal. Fire away!

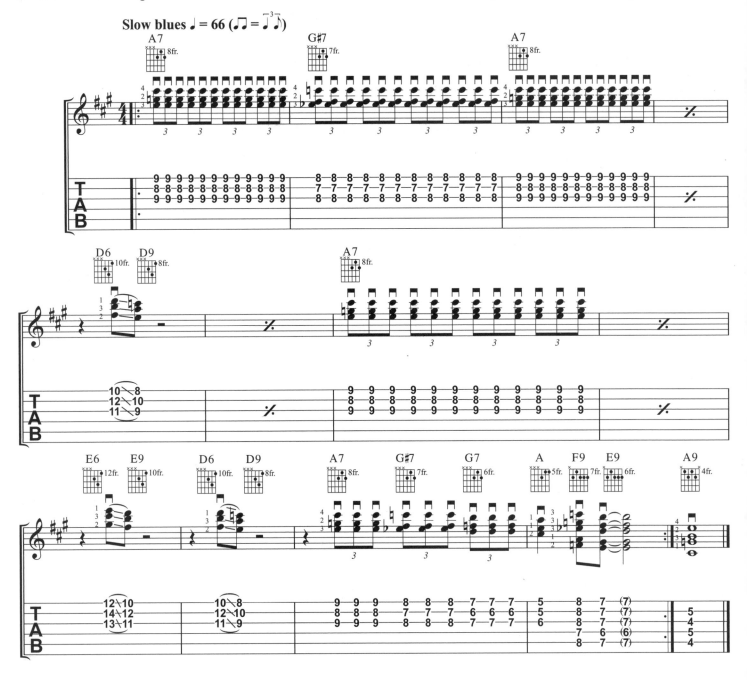

Ways to Make This Example Sound Great

- Play the triplets evenly and pick them very lightly
- Accent the downbeat of each beat slightly louder than the other beats
- Use a clean tone and the neck pickup

Example 3: Yazoo, That's My Baby

This example uses an interval of a 6th. Each measure contains two slides: up and then down. Play the first note, then slide up a whole step. Play the second note (the 6th) and then slide down a whole step. Begin the phrase on beat 2 of each measure. For the turnaround in measure 11, you may play with a pick or use *hybrid picking* by alternating between your pick and middle finger.

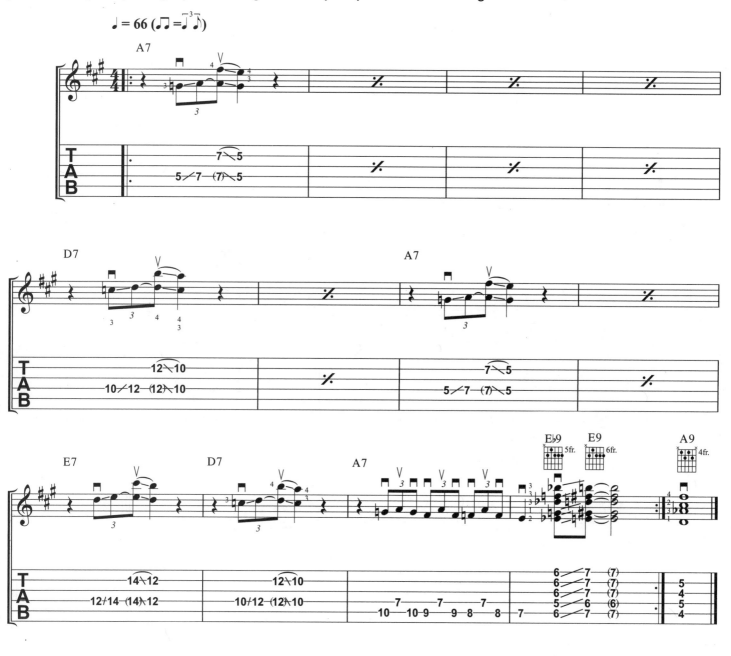

Ways to Make This Example Sound Great

- Allow both strings to ring during the downward slide
- Let the notes ring for their full durations
- Play in a relaxed manner
- Add a slight vibrato to both strings
- Dial in a clean sound with a bit of chorus

Example 4: Closin' Time

This example begins with a whole-step chord slide on strings 3, 2, and 1. The slide begins on beat 2. The E7 and D7 chords also use three-note chord voicings. The turnaround is a single-note blues lick; mixing chords and single notes is a popular technique.

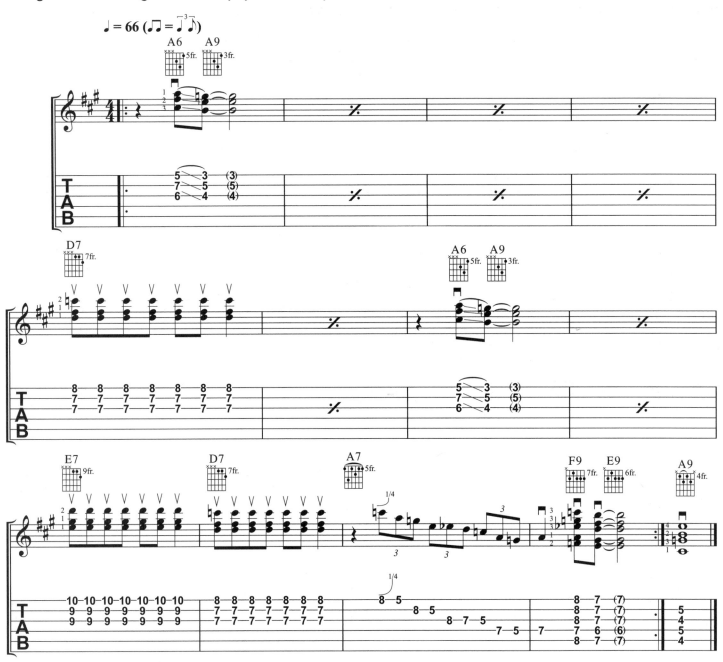

Ways to Make This Example Sound Great

- Pick the chords lightly
- Play the eighth-note triplets in measures 5, 6, 9, and 10 using upstrokes
- Be sure to begin the turnaround lick on beat 2!

Example 5: The Stormy Monday Progression

"Stormy Monday" was written by blues great T-Bone Walker. It features a sophisticated chord progression that includes some new chords we have not discussed yet. Also, it is the first quick-change blues that we will play. Notice several of the chords are approached from a half step above, and check out some of the new chord voicings. The turnaround is a standard slow blues single-note phrase.

The last chord is an E augmented chord. It is a variation of the V7 chord and has become the signature of "Stormy Monday."

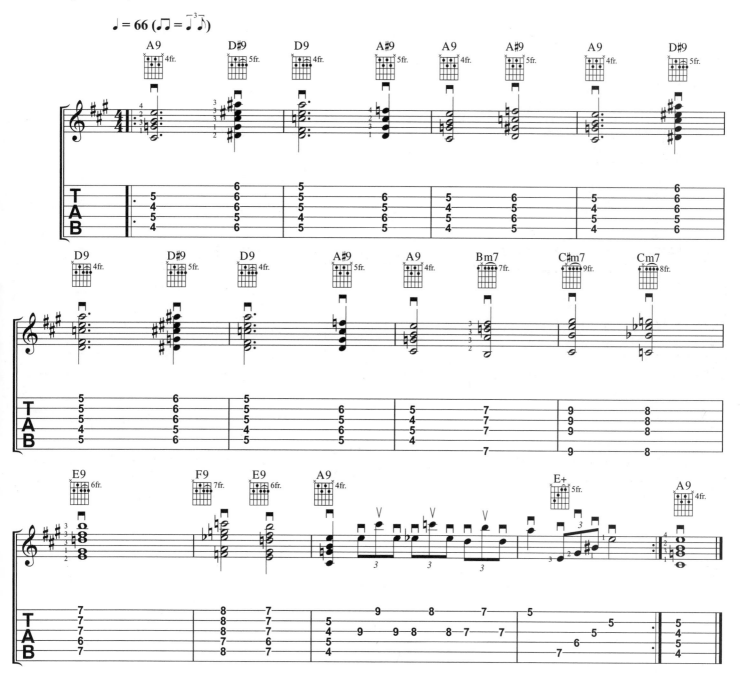

Ways to Make This Example Sound Great

- Strum lightly
- Do not add too much treble or distortion to keep the tone fairly clean and warm
- Play with a relaxed feel

Mambo Blues

The *mambo* rhythm feel is derived from the straight eighth note rather than the shuffle. It has a sound all of its own. A great example of it can be heard on "Crosscut Saw" by Albert King. The mambo is a swampy groove and is a must-know rhythm feel for blues guitarists. What sets this feel apart from the standard straight eighth-note feel is the drums. The mambo is a dance beat that has been adopted by blues artists. Mambo feels may be played as single- note or chord rhythms. This chapter includes examples of both.

The examples in this chapter are in the key of G, ranging from fairly simple to progressively more challenging. Each example contains within it an objective and is designed to demonstrate a specific aspect of mambo blues rhythm.

Example 1: Chordy

This example is played on the backbeat (remember, beats 2 and 4 of each measure). The part should sound like a sharp, percussive "chick." Use only the top four strings. Since the guitar part is essentially doubling the snare drum, it should approximate the same sharpness, duration, and timbre (tone).

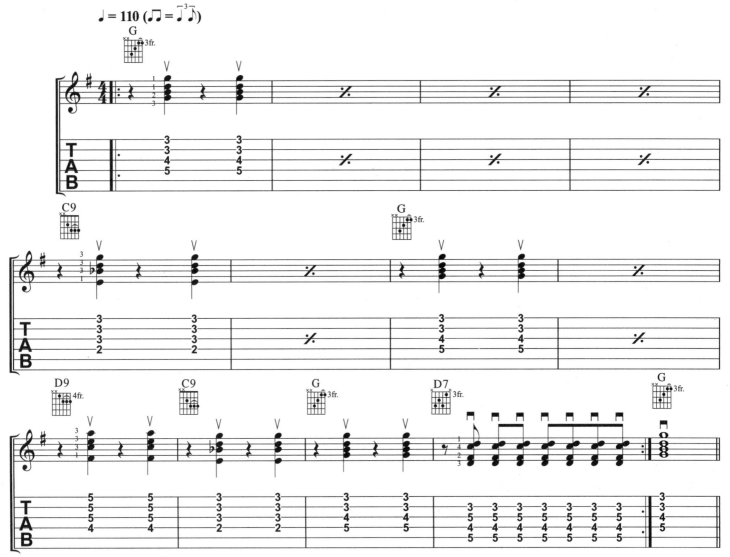

Ways to Make This Example Sound Great

- Use a clean tone and add a bit of reverb
- Use the bridge pickup
- Play the part with your pick using an upstroke

Example 2: Double Cross

This example is a straight eighth-note feel reminiscent of "Crosscut Saw" by Albert King. It is a single-note line that sets up the mambo feel. It sounds great when the bass player of the band doubles it and the drummer plays a rumba or cha-cha beat. The example is designed to mimic what a piano player might play for this type of feel.

Ways to Make This Example Sound Great

- Play in the lowest register possible
- Play using a fairly clean, percussive guitar tone
- Use all downstrokes

Example 3: Shreveport

This single-note rhythm works great for an R&B-style song. It is reminiscent of Wilson Pickett, Sam Cooke, Sam and Dave, and other great R&B artists. This type of rhythm guitar sounds just as contemporary today as it did in the 1960s. It begins with an octave jump followed by a hammer-on that is then repeated down a whole step.

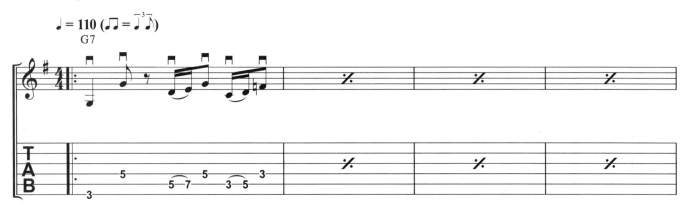

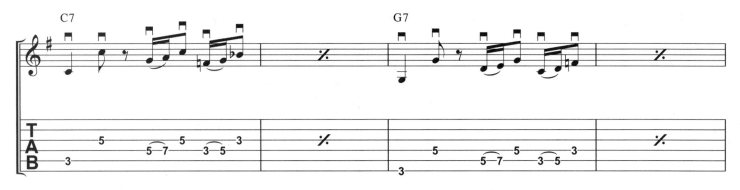

Ways to Make This Example Sound Great

- Play using a very thin tone from the bridge pickup
- Play crisply with all the notes articulated
- Sound the hammer-ons as loud as the picked notes

Example 4: Big Fun

This one is reminiscent of something that would be played by two saxophonists in a horn section. In a horn section, it would probably be played by two saxophones. The double stops are played on strings 2 and 3. Movement is produced by sliding into the two primary notes from a half step below. Make sure the double stops are played staccato (indicated by dots over the notes). Do this by loosening your fretting-hand grip just after you play the notes.

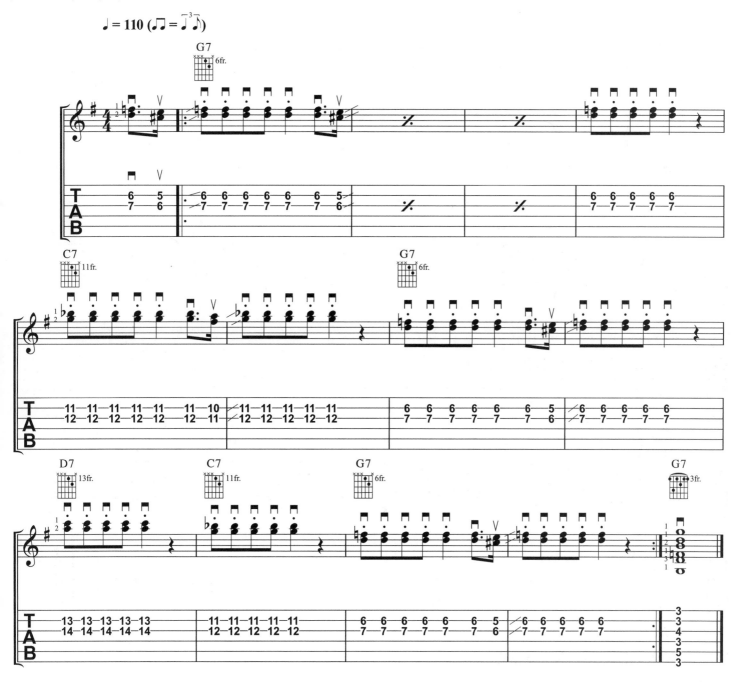

Ways to Make This Example Sound Great

- Use a very clean guitar sound
- Play very staccato
- Choke each double stop just after it is sounded by loosening your grip

Example 5: Waggin'

This example is played on strings 2, 3, and 4 and features a three-note chord. The idea is to play very staccato by loosening your fretting-hand grip just after playing each chord. The movement is produced by resolving the note on the 3rd string down a half step, using the middle finger of your fretting hand.

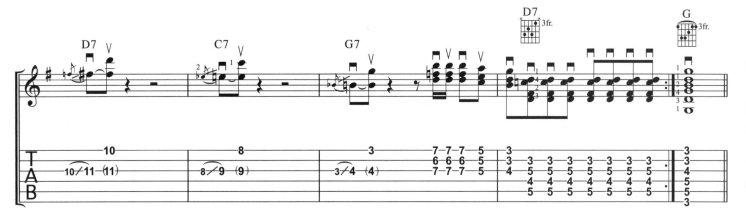

Ways to Make This Example Sound Great

- Play all the chords staccato by lightly loosening your grip just after they are picked
- Play the straight eighth notes evenly and consistently
- Use the neck pickup

Example 6: Jazzeriffic

Notice the more sophisticated, jazzy-sounding chords in this one. The idea is based on dominant 9th chords, and movement is produced by resolving the highest note of each chord down a half step. This is done with your 1st finger. The chord voicings are simply moved up the neck to accommodate the changes. Work on moving your 1st finger while keeping the others fixed.

The chords are very slick and are used to create a more polished sound. Although you may play the entire chord with a pick, it is suggested that you use fingerpicking. Pluck strings 6, 4, 3, and 2 using your thumb, index, middle, and ring fingers respectively.

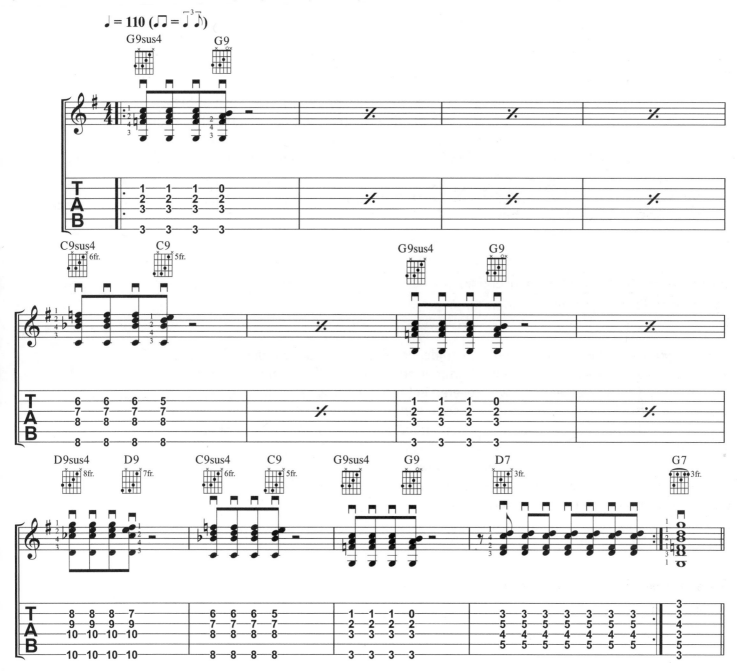

Ways to Make This Example Sound Great

- Play the chords very staccato by loosening your grip just after playing each one
- Use the neck pickup of your guitar
- Try fingerpicking so that all the notes are plucked simultaneously—otherwise use all downstrokes!

SECTION TWO Blues Lead Guitar

Introduction to Blues Lead Guitar

In Section One, we covered some of the most popular blues rhythm styles, now let's learn how to solo over those styles. Developing your own lead guitar voice is an exciting endeavor for all blues guitarists. You'll gain many insights from learning to play transcribed solos and then applying those concepts and techniques to create your own blues solos.

Section Two is highlighted by 18 full-length solos in the styles of blues greats such as Stevie Ray Vaughan, Albert Collins, Eric Clapton, B. B. King, Jimi Hendrix, and Albert King. These solos are presented in various feels, tempos, and keys, and are written in both TAB and standard music notation. You'll be playing over some of the most popular blues rhythm styles, including:

- Medium blues shuffle (in the style of Stevie Ray Vaughan)
- Straight eighth blues-rock (in the style of Chuck Berry)
- Blues-rock shuffle (in the style of Eric Clapton)
- Uptown/jump blues (in the style of B. B. King)
- Slow blues (in the style of Jimi Hendrix)
- Mambo blues (in the style of Albert King)

Section Two begins with a handy reference guide, or refresher, for basic blues lead guitar techniques like bending, slides, pull-offs, hammer-ons, vibrato, trills, the blues rake, and double stops. Though some of this was covered in Section One, we'll examine it here from a lead guitar perspective. Additionally, all the scale patterns necessary to play blues lead guitar are included: the minor pentatonic, major pentatonic, and blues scale. The rest of the section covers individual blues licks and phrases as well as full-length solos in the styles of some of the world's greatest blues guitarists. The ideas and concepts presented in the solos and licks will give you a plethora of ideas to create your own solos. Plus, every solo is performed and broken down on the companion video.

Techniques

The Slide

To perform a slide, play the first note and, while keeping pressure applied on the string, slide up to the second note. The diagonal line shows that it is a slide and not a hammer-on or pull-off.

SLIDE UP

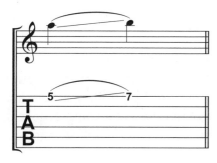

SLIDE DOWN

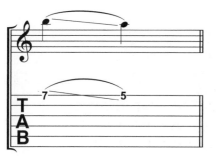

The Pull-Off

To do a pull-off, play the higher note with your first finger already in position on the lower note, then pull your finger off the first note with a strong downward motion that plucks the string, sounding the lower note.

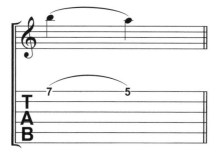

The Hammer-On

To execute a hammer-on, play the lower note, then "hammer" your finger to the higher note. Only the first note is plucked.

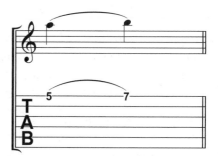

Bending

Bending is probably the most common or popular technique for playing the blues. It means you move one note to a higher one by pushing it up toward the ceiling or by pulling it towards the floor. Bends may be a half step or greater. Some of the great blues-rock players actually bend a note two whole steps, or four frets! Bending requires work and must be practiced slowly. You can use any or all fingers to bend notes, but typically the 3rd or ring finger is the best choice.

HALF-STEP BEND

WHOLE-STEP BEND

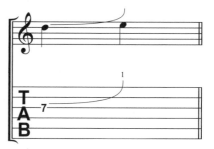

STEP-AND-A-HALF BEND

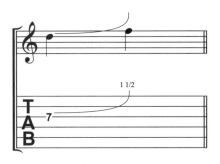

Vibrato

Vibrato is a technique that is used to add movement to a note by using a rapid shaking of the fretting hand, wrist, and forearm. You may use any finger for vibrato, however, the 1st and 3rd fingers are most common.

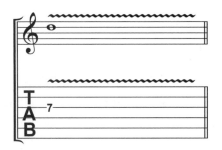

VIBRATO AT THE TOP OF A BENT NOTE

You may also add vibrato at the top of a bend. Bend a note to the desired pitch and add vibrato.

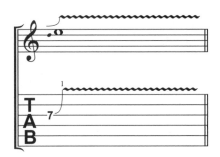

The Trill

A trill is when you rapidly alternate between two notes using a succession of hammer-ons and pull-offs.

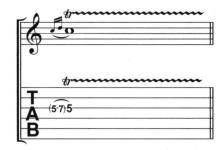

The Rake

The rake is a great technique for giving your solo attitude. It is performed by fretting a note and then "raking" across the remaining strings; make sure to palm mute the remaining "raked" strings you are not fretting.

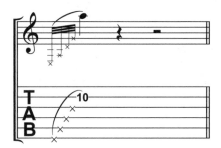

Scales

The main scales used in this book are:

- The minor pentatonic scale (scale degrees: 1-♭3-4-5-♭7)
- The blues scale (1-♭3-4-♭5-♮5-♭7)
- The major pentatonic scale (1-2-3-5-6)

These are mostly moveable patterns, which means they may be transposed to any key by identifying the tonic tones of each pattern and moving the scale fingering up or down the fretboard.

Scale Variations

You'll also find scale patterns for the minor and major pentatonic scales with variations. These variations will add color to your solos.

MINOR PENTATONIC

Here are five patterns for the minor pentatonic scale in the key of A. The hollow dots [o] represent the roots of the chords.

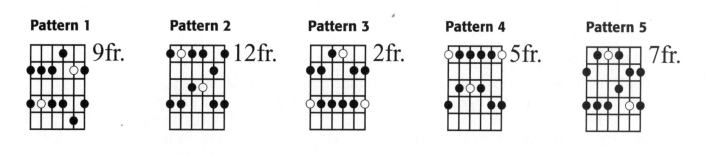

BLUES SCALE

Here are five patterns for the blues scale in the key of A.

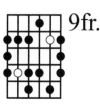

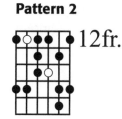
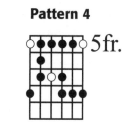
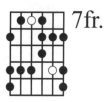

MAJOR PENTATONIC

Here are five patterns for the major pentatonic scale in the key of A.

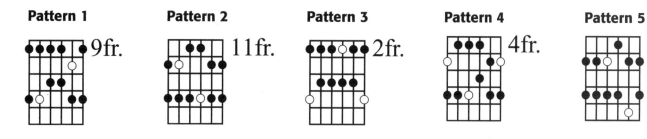

MINOR PENTATONIC SCALE WITH CHROMATIC NOTES

Here is an example of the minor pentatonic scale with chromatic notes in the key of A.

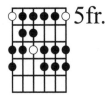
5fr.

MAJOR PENTATONIC WITH CHROMATIC NOTES

Here is an example of the major pentatonic scale with chromatic notes in the key of A.

2fr.

The 1x12 Soloing Concept

In this book, you'll learn how to play blues lead using the concept of *1x12*. This unique idea teaches you to play one lick that repeats three times during one 12-bar *chorus* of the blues. (A chorus is one cycle through the 12-bar blues.) These licks will focus on the techniques learned throughout this book. Because the 1x12 concept uses one lick that is repeated three times, you will reinforce the traditional call and response effect that characterizes the blues. This will help your solos sound more cohesive and fluid.

The 1x12 concept also helps with memorizing a lick or idea through repetition. It will help you think of each 12-bar form (one chorus) as a short story, as if it were a conversation taking place between two people. The repetition of the 1x12 idea will help the listener to hear your solo in a logical and lyrical way. The story you tell will have a beginning, middle, and end.

Medium Shuffle
(In the Style of Stevie Ray Vaughan)

Stevie Ray Vaughan, affectionately known as "SRV," is one of the most influential guitarists of the 20th century. He brought the blues back into mainstream popularity with his ferocious playing, good songwriting, and impassioned vocals. His classic songs, "Pride and Joy," "Texas Flood," and "Crossfire," feature some of the greatest blues lead guitar playing ever.

Objective

- Learn how to solo over a blues shuffle in the key of E
- Learn how to play a pattern for the blues scale in the key of E
- Learn to play 13 blues licks in the style of Stevie Ray Vaughan
- Learn to play solos in the style of Stevie Ray Vaughan

Scale Pattern Used in This Chapter: E Blues Scale

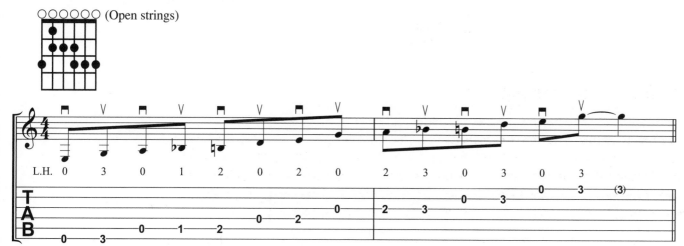

NOTE: This pattern is not moveable due to the inclusion of open strings.

Medium Shuffle Licks

The following are 13 medium shuffle blues licks in the style of Stevie Ray Vaughan. As usual with the blues, swing the eighth notes when you play.

LICK 1

This example uses double stops. Play the 2nd string at the 5th fret together with the 1st string open. Strum using downstrokes with a strong shuffle feel.

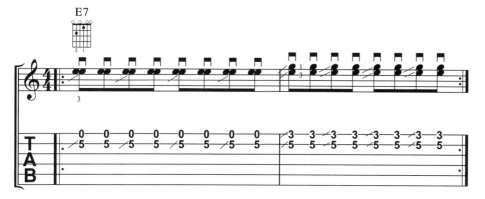

LICK 2

Here, we have octaves and a grace note. The grace note has no time value and is used to slide into the 2nd fret of the 3rd string from a whole step above.

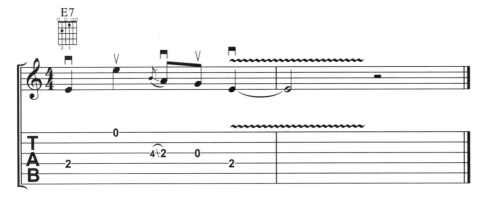

LICK 3

Begin with double stops, and strum using downstrokes.

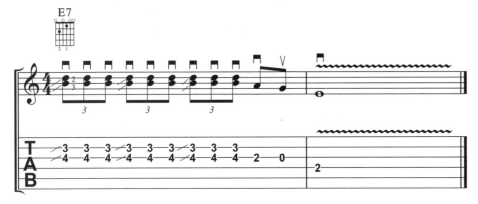

LICK 4

Play this bass-note run with downstrokes. Playing blues scales in the lower octaves is a Stevie Ray Vaughan trademark.

LICK 5

Adding chromatic tones to the blues scale in the low register is another SRV signature.

LICK 6

Here is another bass run that incorporates the 3rd string.

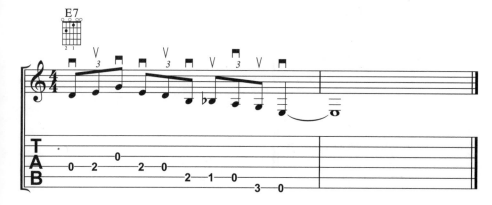

LICK 7

Use a trill on the 3rd string for this classic blues riff.

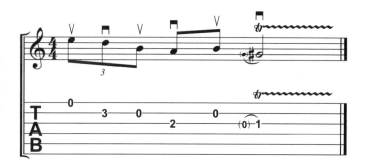

LICK 8

Notice the chromatic notes in this classic bass-note run.

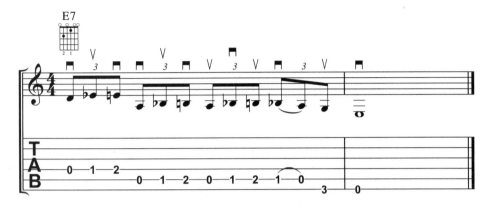

LICK 9

Play the ascending and descending slide with your middle finger.

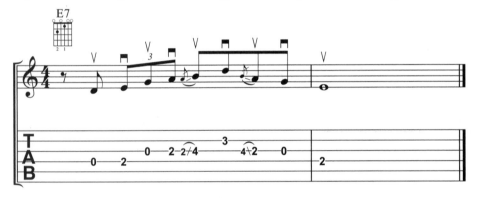

LICK 10

This workhorse lick features chromatic notes on the 2nd and 3rd strings.

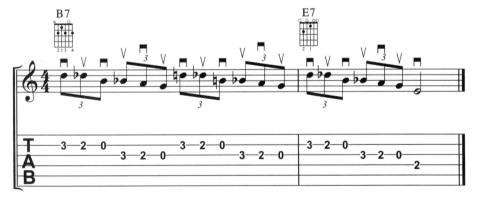

LICK 11

This example includes double stops and chromatic notes. Play the double stops using your 3rd and 2nd fingers.

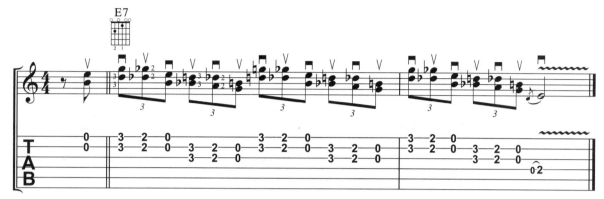

LICK 12

Like the example above, this double-stop lick mixes the blues scale with chromatic notes.

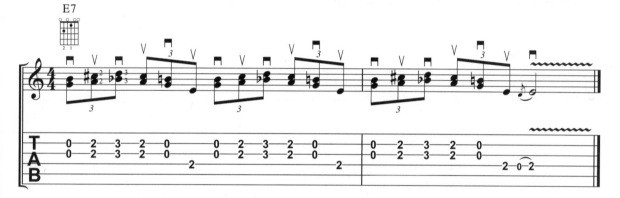

LICK 13

This example combines ascending and descending double stops and features chromatic notes.

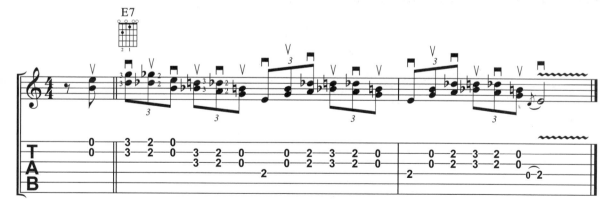

Medium Shuffle Solos

Below are three medium shuffle solos in the style of Stevie Ray Vaughan using the 1x12 concept. Each solo incorporates one or more of the licks discussed in this chapter. The solos are broken down in detail in the video.

SOLO 1

SOLO 2

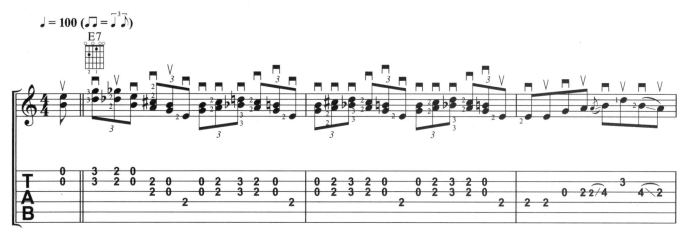

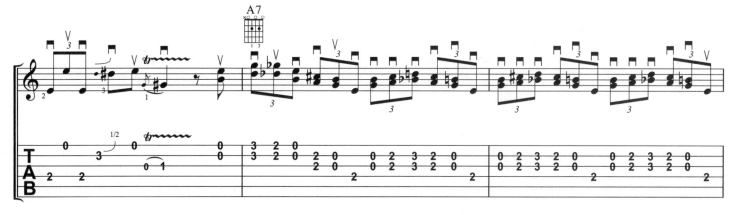

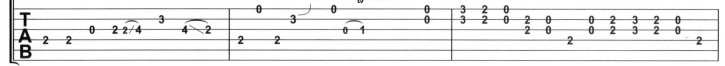

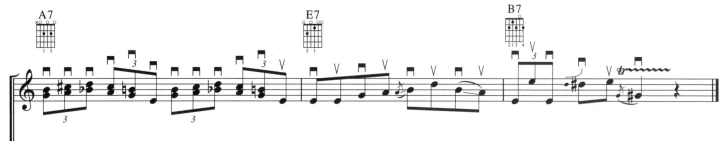

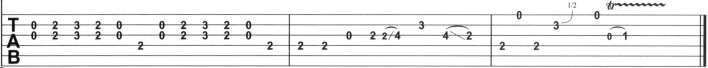

SOLO 3

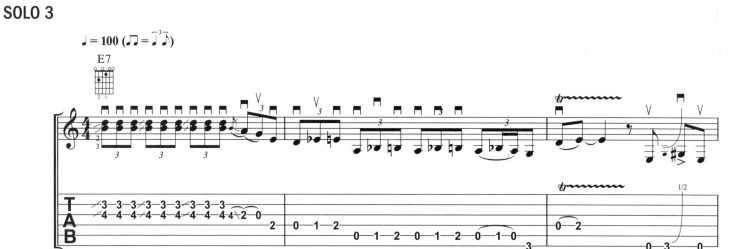

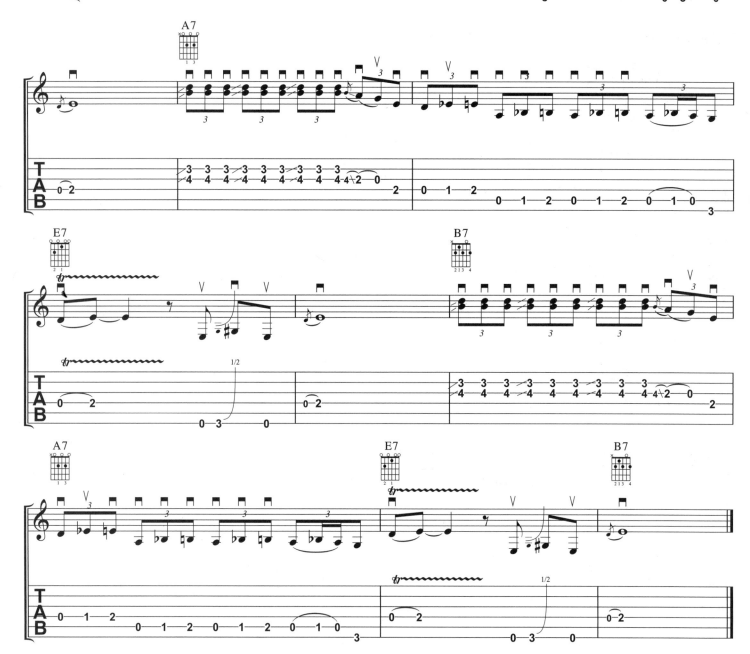

Funky Straight Eighths
(In the Style of Albert Collins)

Albert Collins, called "The Ice Man," was known for his emotional and fierce guitar playing. His classic songs are "Frosty," "Get Your Business Straight," and "Don't Lose Your Cool."

Objective
- Learn how to solo over a funky blues in the key of C
- Learn how to play a pattern for the blues scale and the major pentatonic in the key of C
- Combine the major pentatonic scale with the blues scale to create new sounds
- Learn to play 17 blues licks in the style of Albert Collins
- Learn to play solos in the style of Albert Collins

Scale Patterns Used in This Chapter: C Blues Scale

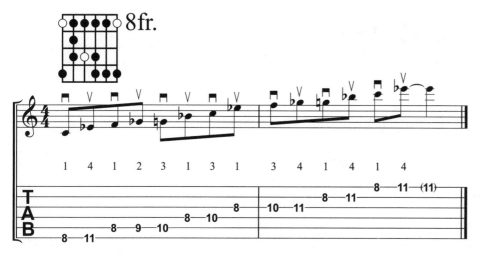

C Major Pentatonic Scale

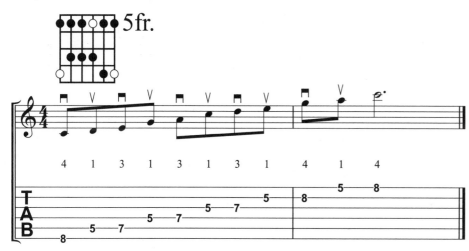

Funky Straight Eighths Licks

Here are 17 funky straight eighths blues licks in the style of Albert Collins.

LICK 1

This example uses a double-stop bend and double stops.

LICK 2

This lick features a position shift in the first measure and borrows notes from the blues scale.

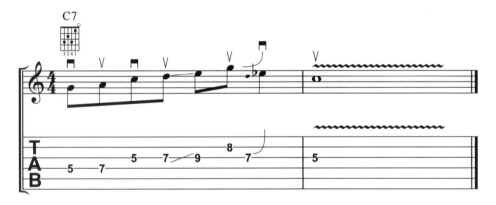

LICK 3

This example shifts from the blues scale to the major pentatonic. The position shift occurs in measure 2.

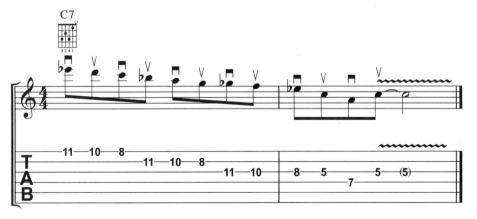

LICK 4

This example also shifts from the blues scale to the major pentatonic. A position shift occurs in measure 2.

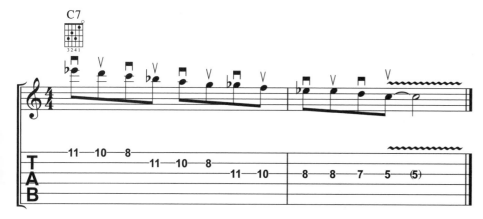

LICK 5

This lick moves from the major pentatonic to the blues scale. Check out the TAB for the position shift.

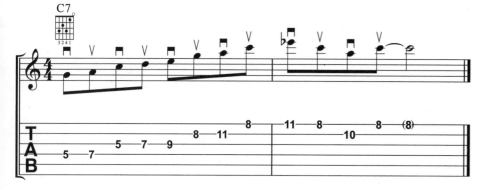

LICK 6

The example below focuses on using pull-offs in the blues scale and includes a position shift.

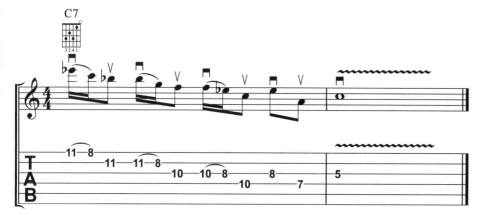

LICK 7

This example shifts positions from the major pentatonic scale to the blues scale.

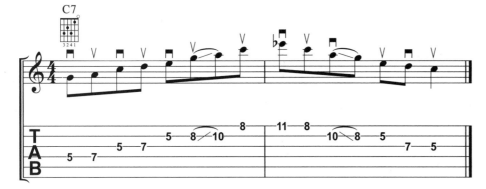

LICK 8

In this example, you'll slide on the 2nd string to transition from the major pentatonic to the blues scale and back.

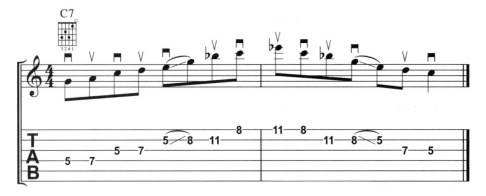

LICK 9

This example features a position shift using a slide on the 3rd string.

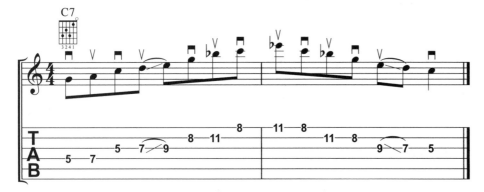

LICK 10
This example features half-step and whole-step slides.

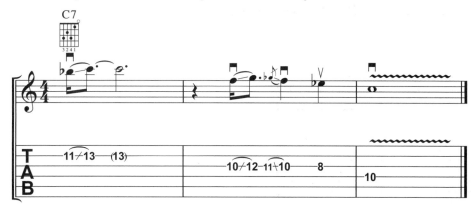

LICK 11
This example features slides and a half-step bend.

LICK 12
This example features the major pentatonic scale plus hammer-ons and pull-offs.

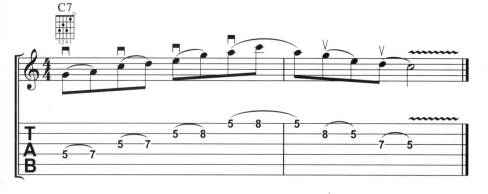

LICK 13
The following lick demonstrates the major pentatonic using all hammer-ons.

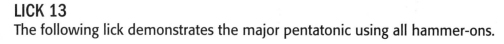
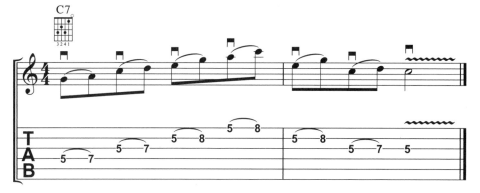

LICK 14
Here's a great blues phrase in the minor pentatonic scale using hammer-ons.

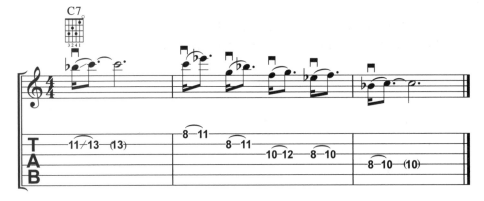

LICK 15
Below is another great blues phrase in the minor pentatonic scale incorporating a bend and hammer-ons.

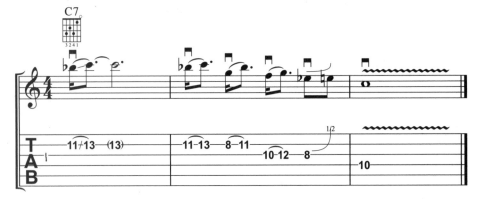

LICK 16
Let's now descend the major pentatonic scale using pull-offs.

LICK 17
Next, we descend the blues scale using pull-offs. The position shift happens on string 5.

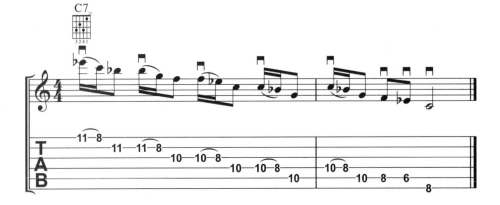

Funky Straight Eighths Solos

Below are three funky straight eighths solos in the style of Albert Collins that use the 1x12 concept. Each solo incorporates one or more of the licks discussed in this chapter. Follow along with Steve Trovato as he plays these solos in the video.

SOLO 1

* **m** means to play with the middle finger of your right (picking) hand

---

SOLO 2

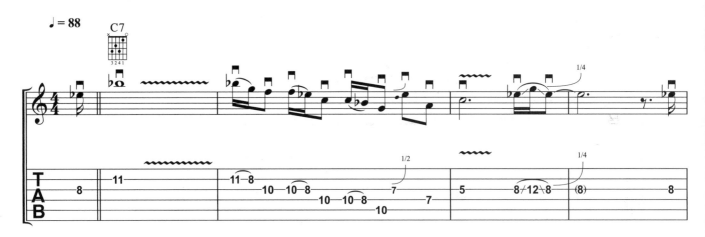

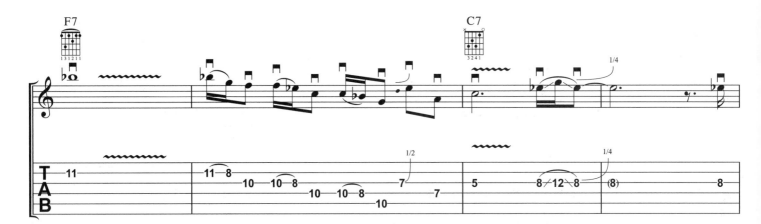

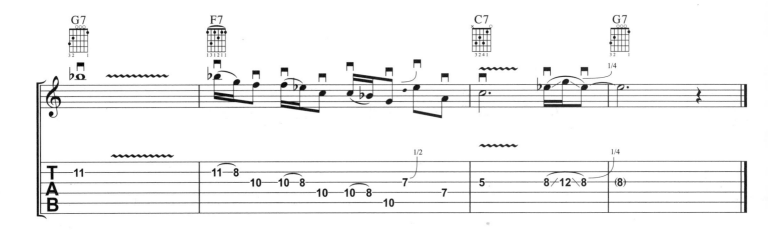

SOLO 3

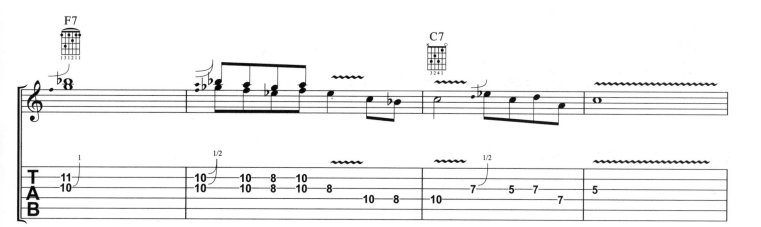

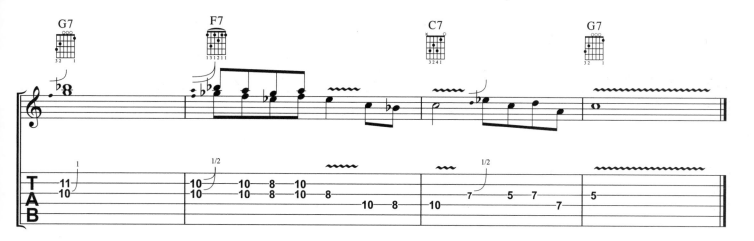

Blues-Rock
(In the Style of Eric Clapton)

Eric Clapton's career has spanned over five decades. He emerged as one of the top blues-rock guitarists in the 1960s with his band Cream. Moving through the decades, with dozens of albums and numerous hit songs, Clapton became a fixture in the blues as both a performer and historian. His blues lead guitar skills are almost without equal.

Objective

- Learn to solo over blues-rock shuffle in the key of A
- Learn a pattern for the blues scale in the key of A
- Learn how to play short, repetitious blues phrases
- Learn to use hammer-ons and pull-offs in blues soloing
- Learn how to sequence the minor pentatonic scale to create blues-rock runs
- Learn to play 11 blues licks in the style of Eric Clapton
- Learn to play solos in the style of Eric Clapton

Scale Pattern Used in This Chapter: A Minor Pentatonic Scale

Blues-Rock Licks

The following are 11 blues-rock licks in the style of Eric Clapton. Play them all with a shuffle feel.

LICK 1

In this lick, the phrase starts with a pickup note. Bend notes on the 1st and 2nd strings slightly to achieve effective half-step bends. Notice that repeating the phrase builds momentum and energy.

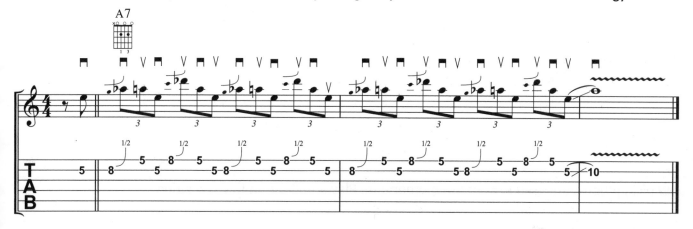

LICK 2

Start with a half-step bend on the 3rd string. Bend using your 3rd finger and support the bend with your 2nd finger. Using two fingers for a bend will help to control the bend and maintain pitch.

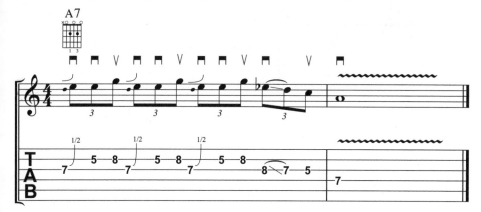

LICK 3

Here, you will be pulling off from the 7th fret to the 5th fret of the 3rd string.

LICK 4

This lick includes both a pull-off and a hammer-on.

LICK 5

Notice how pickup notes are used to start the momentum. Play a pull-off on the 2nd string.

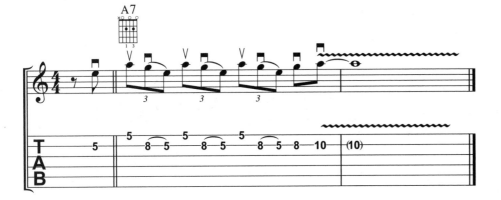

LICK 6

This short phrase is a rockin' blues workhorse. Barre strings 1 and 2 at the 5th fret, then bend the note on the 3rd string using your 3rd finger, supporting the bend with your 2nd finger for added control.

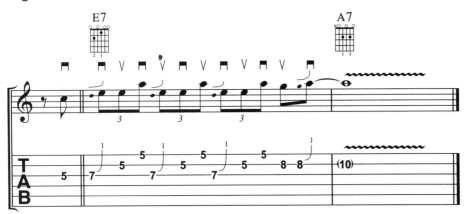

LICK 7

Set up the phrase by barring the top two strings at the 5th fret. Begin with a bend on the 3rd string.
Play the lick with all downstrokes.

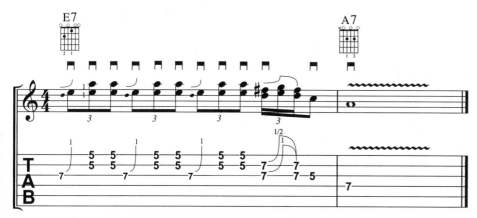

LICK 8

Here's a great ascending lick using a three-note sequence from the minor pentatonic scale.

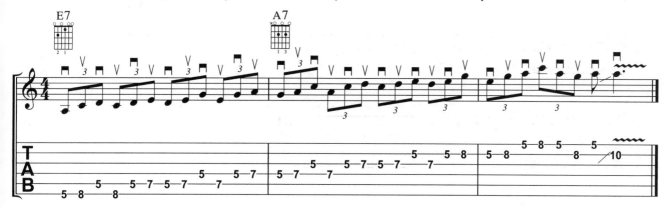

LICK 9

Below is another example of pentatonic sequencing. Although it is still a group-of-three sequence,
the notes are ordered differently here.

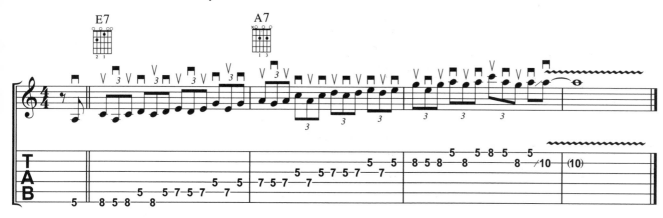

LICK 10

This is a cool lick that features both hammer-ons and pull-offs. It is in a group-of-six sequence.
Practice this very slowly and master it before playing up to tempo.

LICK 11

This is a group-of-three, call and response sequence. The call is ascending, and the response is descending.

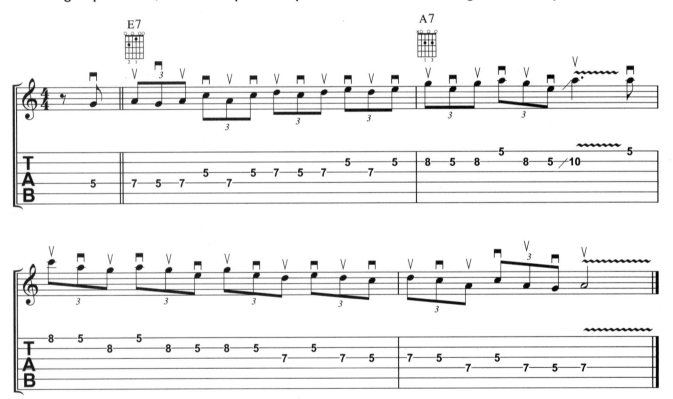

Blues-Rock Solos

Below are three blues-rock solos in the style of Eric Clapton that incorporate the 1x12 concept. Each solo features one or more of the licks discussed in this chapter; all three solos are performed and broken down in the video.

SOLO 1

SOLO 2

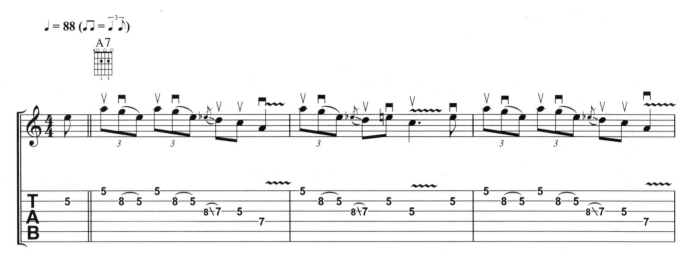

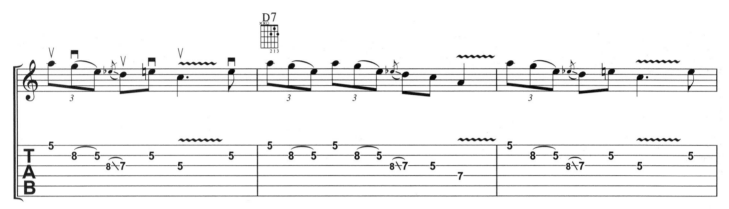

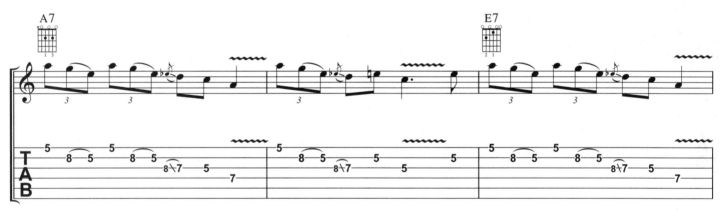

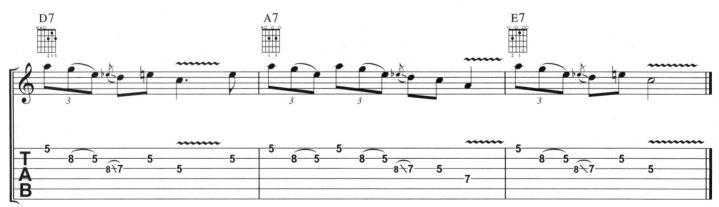

SOLO 3

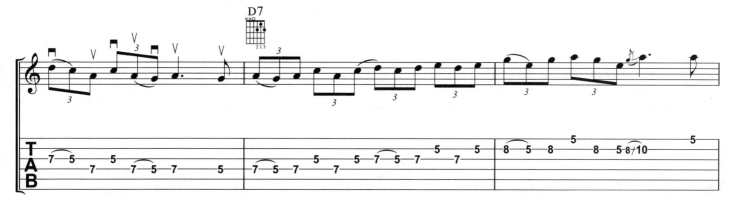

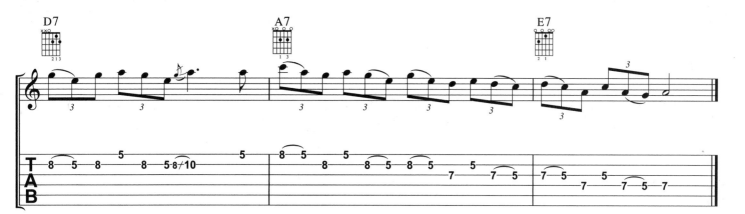

Uptown/Jump Blues

(In the Style of B. B. King)

B. B. King is probably the most beloved blues musician of all time. He has been inducted into the Rock and Roll Hall of Fame and has won several Grammy awards. His sweet, lyrical guitar playing has become one of the most recognizable sounds in blues.

Objective

- Learn how to play a blues shuffle in the key of G
- Learn a pattern for the blues scale and for the major pentatonic scale
- Learn to combine the blues scale and the major pentatonic scale to create new blues ideas
- Learn 11 blues licks in the style of B. B. King
- Learn to play solos in the style of B. B. King

Scale Pattern Used in This Chapter:
The G Major Pentatonic Scale (with Position Shift) in the 7th Position

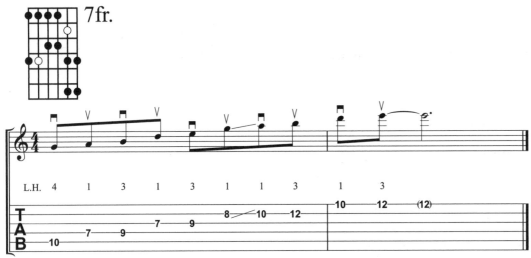

The G Blues Scale (with Position Shift) in the 10th Position

Uptown/Jump Blues Licks

The following are 11 uptown/jump blues licks in the style of B. B. King. Play them with a shuffle feel.

LICK 1

This example begins with three pickup notes. Check out the TAB for the fingering and position shift.

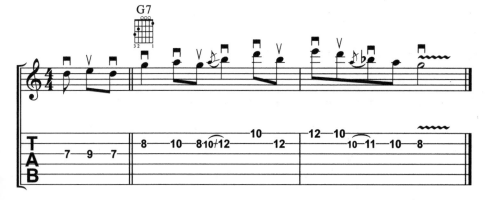

LICK 2

This lick begins with a slide on the 2nd string. Notice the underlying shuffle feel in this example.

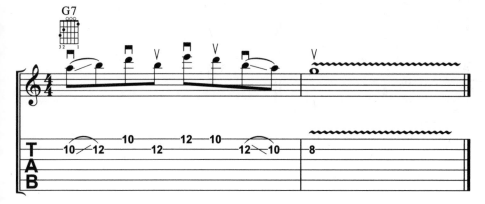

LICK 3

This example features half-step slides. Watch the TAB for position shifts and fingering.

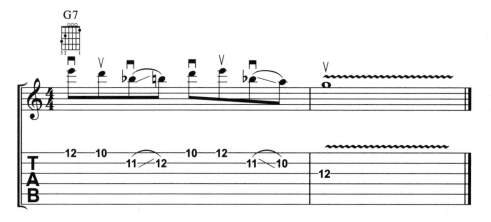

LICK 4

This major pentatonic idea features pull-offs on strings 1 and 2.

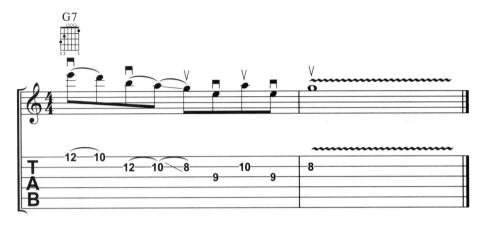

LICK 5

This lick uses the major pentatonic scale and a half-step bend on string 2.

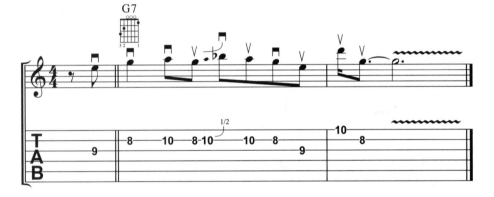

LICK 6

This example mixes the blues scale with the major pentatonic scale. It contains two ideas strung together with a position shift. The first measure is the major pentatonic scale, and the second measure shifts up to the blues scale. Notice the lick begins on beat 2 and features a half-step and a whole-step bend.

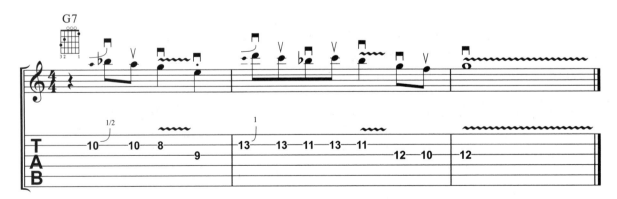

LICK 7

Here is a great blues lick that has "B. B. King" written all over it. Watch for the half-step and whole-step bends.

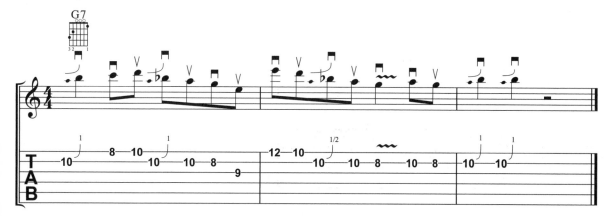

LICK 8

This example features a combination of major and minor pentatonic scales and half-step bends.

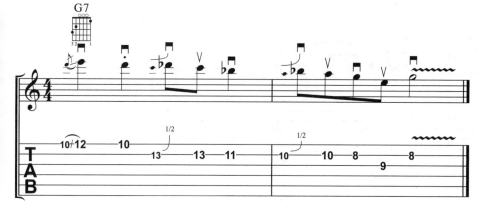

LICK 9

This lick is a repetitious phrase that includes a hammer-on and pull-off.

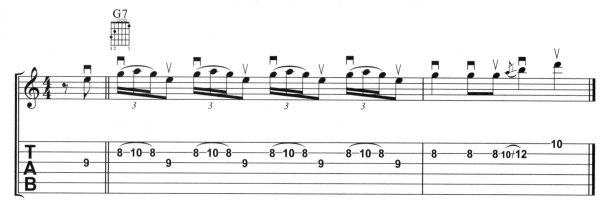

LICK 10

Here is a lick that's chock full of ideas. Shift positions using a slide on the 3rd string.
Also, notice the chromatic notes in measure 2.

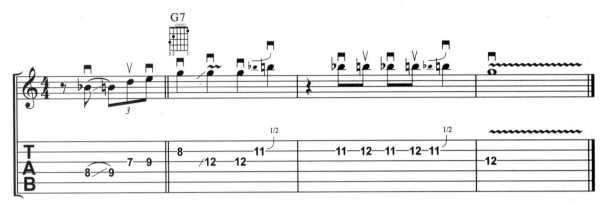

LICK 11

This example uses both the major and the minor pentatonic scales. Check out the TAB
for position shifts and bends.

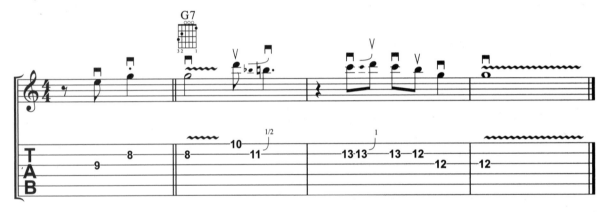

Uptown/Jump Blues Solos

Below are three uptown/jump blues solos in the style of B. B. King that use the 1x12 concept. Each solo incorporates one or more of the concepts and licks discussed in this chapter. Watch Steve perform and teach the solos in the video.

SOLO 1

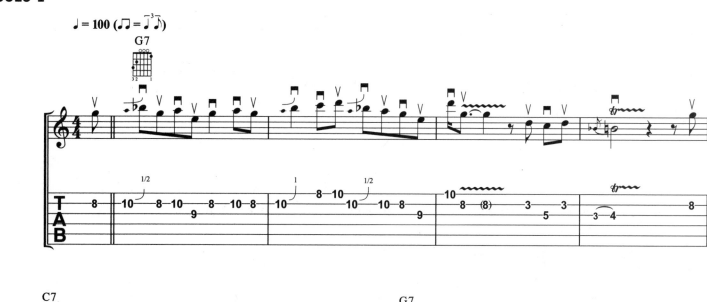

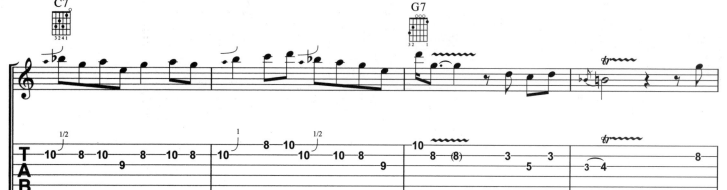

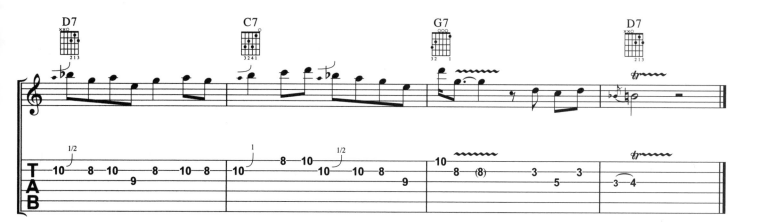

SOLO 2

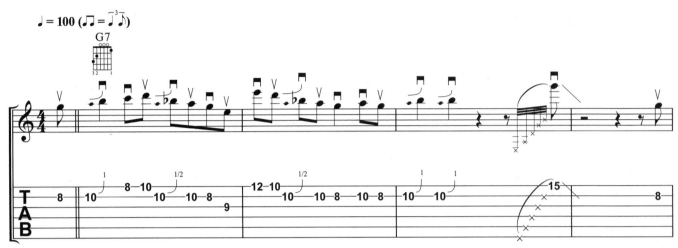

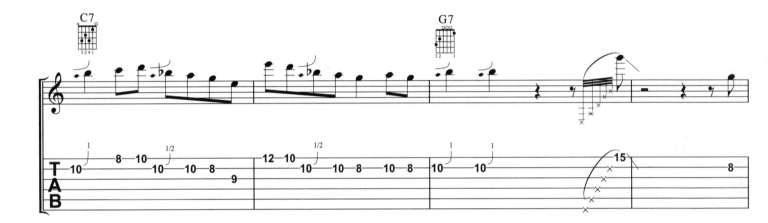

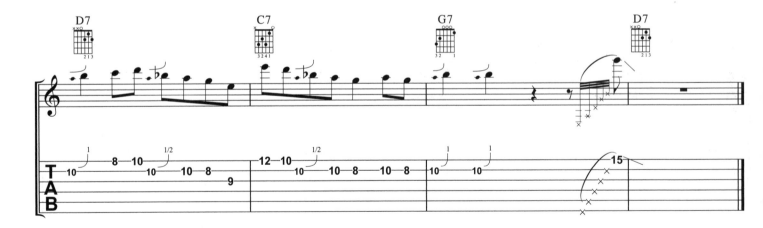

SOLO 3

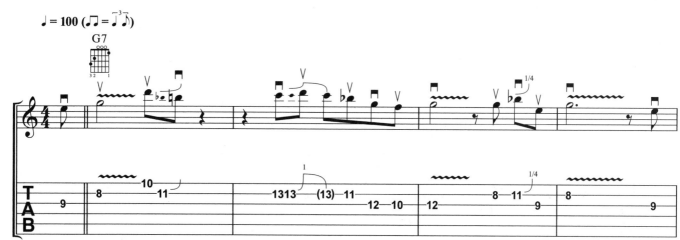

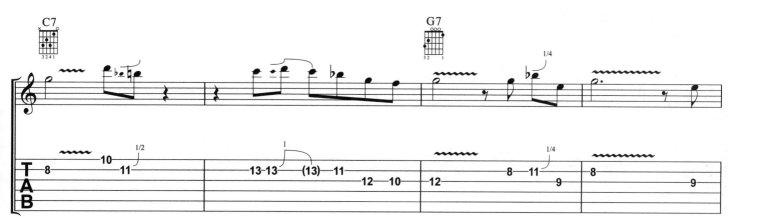

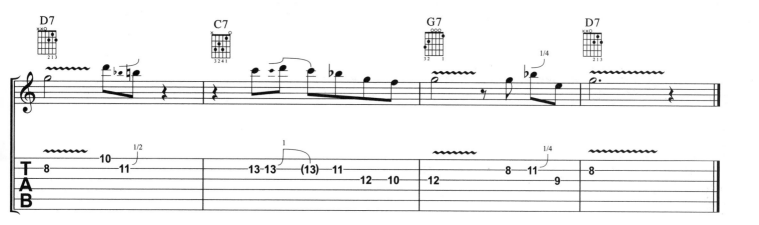

Slow Blues
(In the Style of Jimi Hendrix)

Jimi Hendrix is one of the best-known and most-influential guitarists of all time. He added a rock element to traditional blues and created a new, aggressive, and raw style. His unique lead guitar style is unmistakable.

Objective

- Learn how to play a slow blues in the key of A
- Learn two patterns for the blues scale in the key of A; Pattern 4 and 5
- Learn more about bending notes and the blues rake
- Learn how to use phrase repetition to create great blues riffs
- Learn to play 12 blues licks in the style of Jimi Hendrix
- Learn to play solos in the style of Jimi Hendrix

Scale Pattern Used in This Chapter:
The A Blues Scale in the 5th Position

The A Blues Scale in the 7th Position

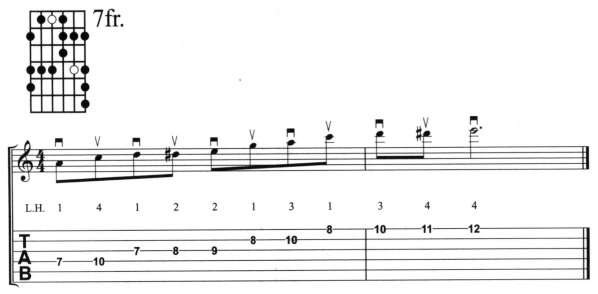

Slow Blues Licks

Let's learn 12 slow blues licks in the style of Jimi Hendrix.

LICK 1

This one uses a bend, a rake, and vibrato. Bend with your 2nd finger supporting your 3rd.

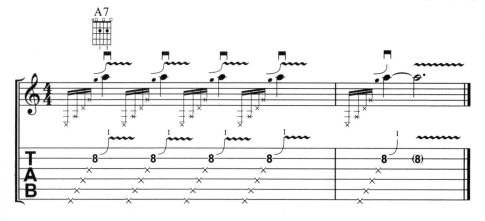

LICK 2

This lick includes a bend while adding vibrato on string 3.

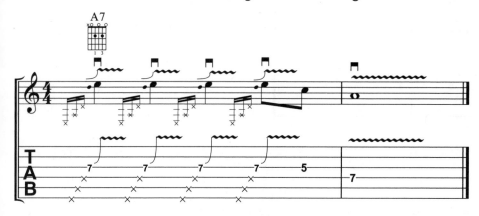

LICK 3

Here is a typical Hendrix idea that is played on the top three strings, featuring bends and a strong vibrato.

LICK 4

This example ends with a short pull-off riff that is typical of blues players.

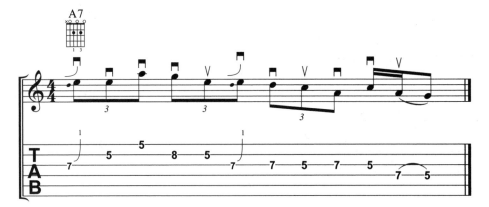

LICK 5

Here is a repetitious idea with a bent note at the end. Remember to add vibrato to the last note.

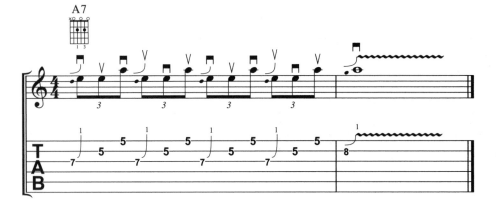

LICK 6

Here is our first position-shift idea. On beat 4, slide up to the 10th fret on the 2nd string.

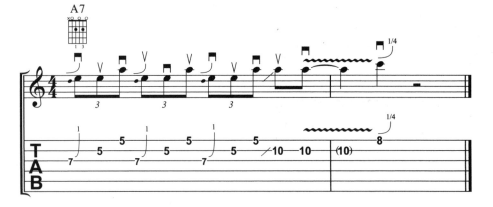

LICK 7

In this lick, bend the 1st string up a whole step at the 10th fret and don't forget the vibrato.

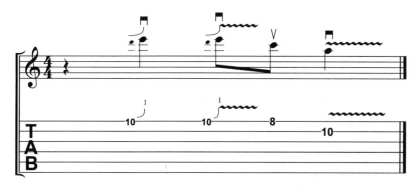

LICK 8

Watch for the whole-step slide on the 3rd string in this example.

LICK 9

In this one, connect the position shift with a slide.

LICK 10

This is a sneaky lick that starts on beat 2 and is in the middle register of the blues scale.

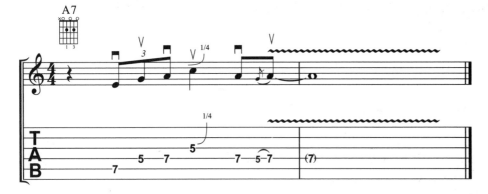

LICK 11

Start this descending run on beat 2 and end on the major 3rd.

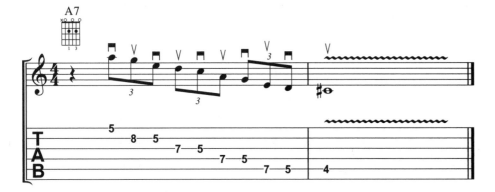

LICK 12

Here is a descending blues scale that starts on beat 2 and incudes a hammer-on.

Slow Blues Solos

Following are three slow blues solos in the style of Hendrix that use the 1x12 concept. The solos incorporate one or more of the licks discussed in this chapter, and are performed and broken down in the video.

SOLO 1

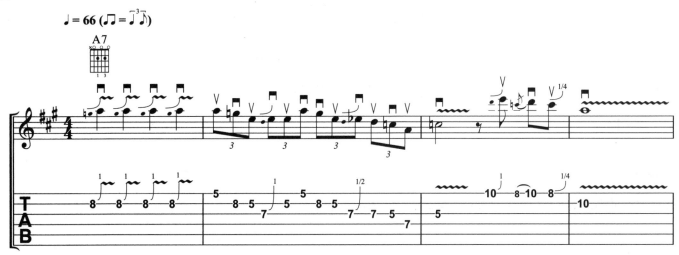

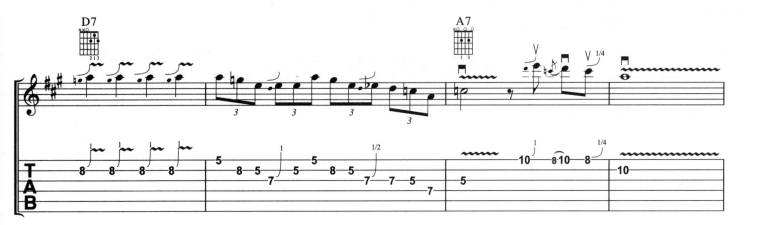

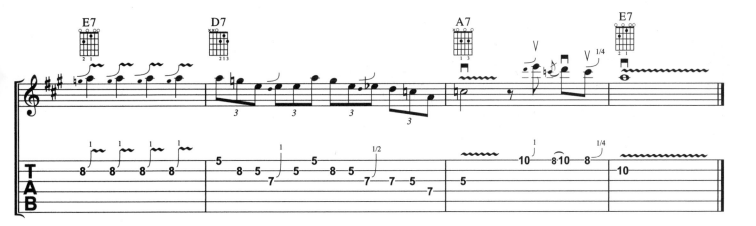

SOLO 2

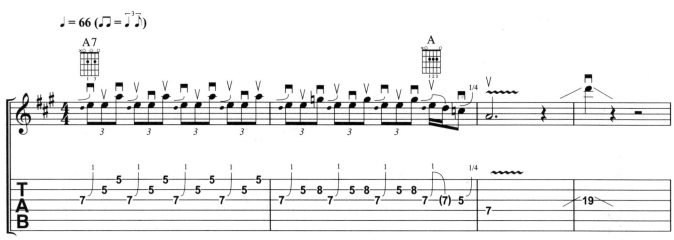

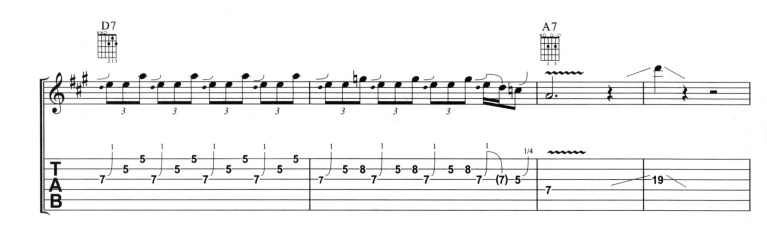

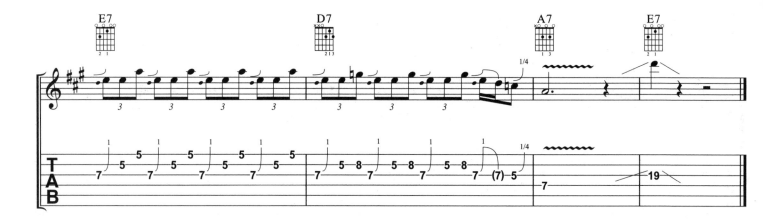

SOLO 3

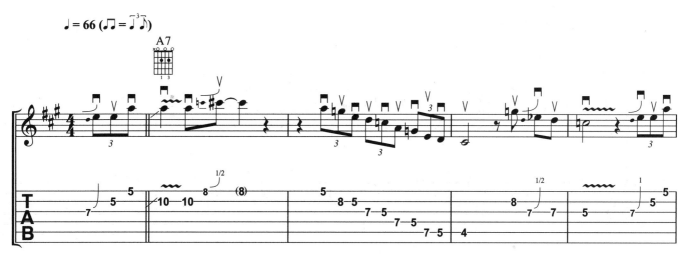

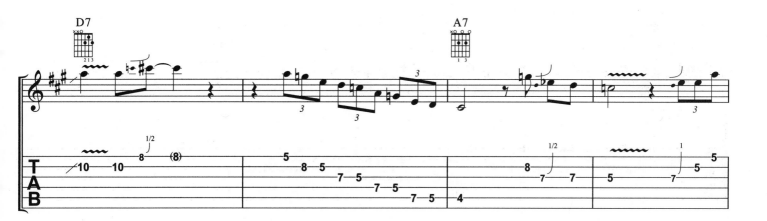

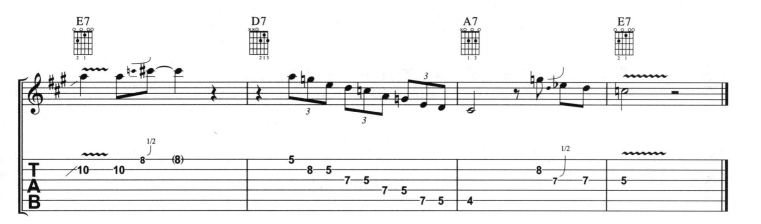

Mambo Blues
(In the Style of Albert King)

Known as the "Velvet Bulldozer," Albert King's aggressive and immense sound is instantly recognizable. His hit songs include "Crosscut Saw," "Blues Power," and "Born Under a Bad Sign."

Objective

- Learn to play a mambo blues feel in the key of G
- Learn a pattern for the blues scale in the key of G
- Learn to borrow notes from other patterns to create blues licks
- Learn the Albert King signature glissando and vibrato
- Learn to play 10 blues licks in the style of Albert King
- Learn to play solos in the style of Albert King

Scale Patterns Used in This Chapter:
G Blues Scale

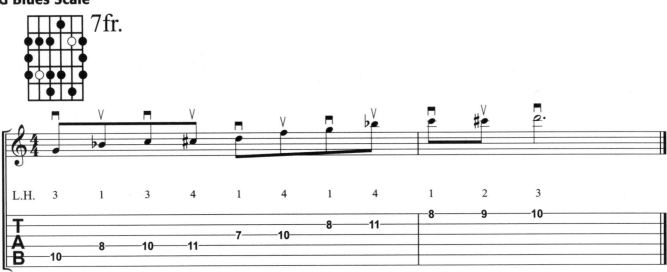

G Blues Scale

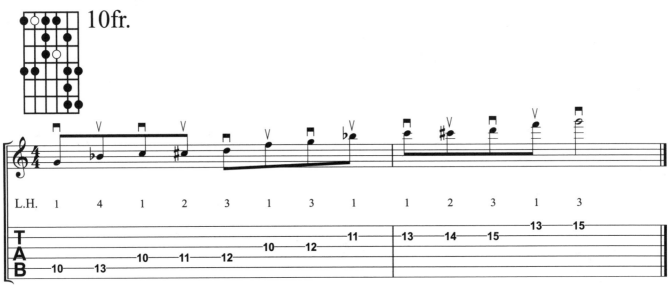

Mambo Blues Licks

Following are 10 mambo blues licks in the style of Albert King.

LICK 1

Here's an idea that moves between several positions of the blues scale and has a half-step bend in the second measure.

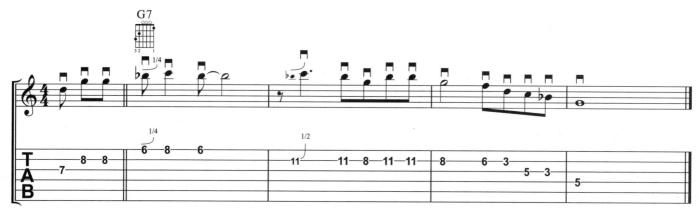

LICK 2

This might be the number one blues lick of all time! It's played on the 1st and 2nd strings. The whole-step bend is from C to D on the 1st string. Be sure to support your bending finger with a least one other finger. Watch the video example for proper phrasing. Blues is all about attitude, so be sure to add some vibrato to the bent note and to the last note of the phrase. Also, try playing this using your fingers instead of a pick!

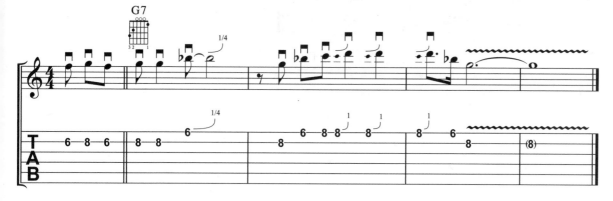

LICK 3

Here is a nasty, classic blues lick. Watch for the hammer-on in measure 1 and don't hurt yourself!

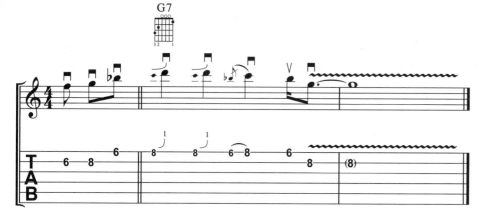

LICK 4

This is a slinky lick with a 3rd-finger bend and a 1st-finger bend that can be quite
challenging. The lick is played on the 2nd and 3rd strings.

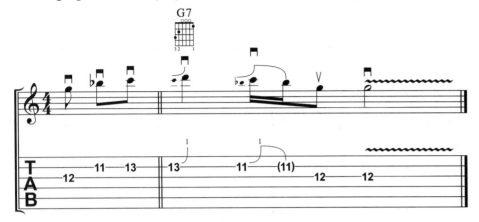

LICK 5

Here is a really cool lick that uses two *pre-bends*. To pre-bend a note means that you bend it
before you actually play it. Play the bent note, then allow it to fall to its original pitch. The pre-bends
in this example are on the 2nd string. Listen for the pickup notes to help with context and phrasing.

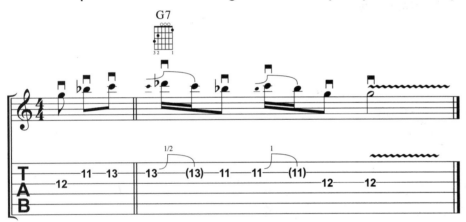

LICK 6

In this example, watch for the hammer-on and pull-off in the first phrase. The last note is the signature
Albert King glissando. Testify!

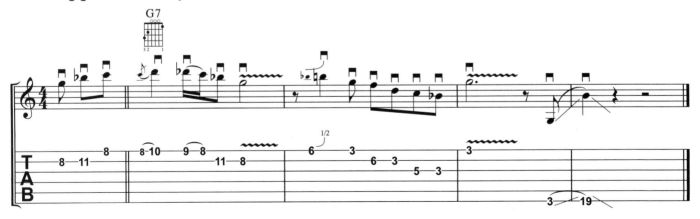

LICK 7

This lick is subtle in that it uses chromatic notes. Play the chromatic note on the ascending phrase, but bend the chromatic note on the descending phrase.

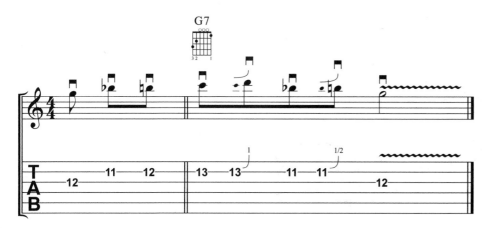

LICK 8

Bend on the 2nd string and then play a note on the 1st string while holding the bend. This idea uses the notes from the G minor pentatonic scale.

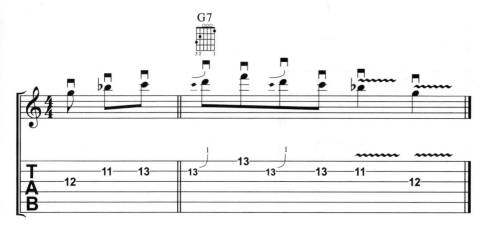

LICK 9

The bend on the 2nd string is played against a note on the 1st string. Let them ring together as a double stop.

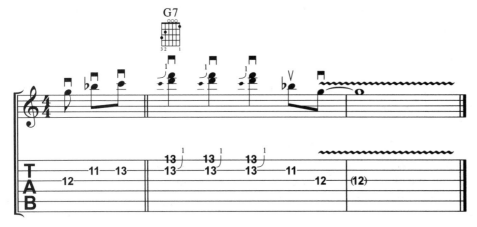

LICK 10

Here is an essential blues lick played in the 3rd position, opening with a slide.

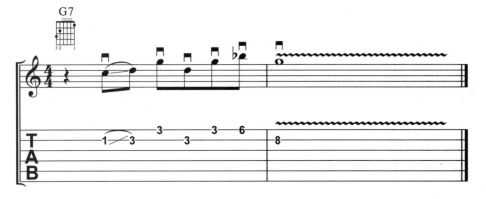

Mambo Blues Solos

Following are three mambo blues solos in the style of Albert King that use the 1x12 concept. Each solo incorporates one or more of the licks discussed in this chapter. Follow along with Steve as performs and breaks down the solos in the video.

SOLO 1

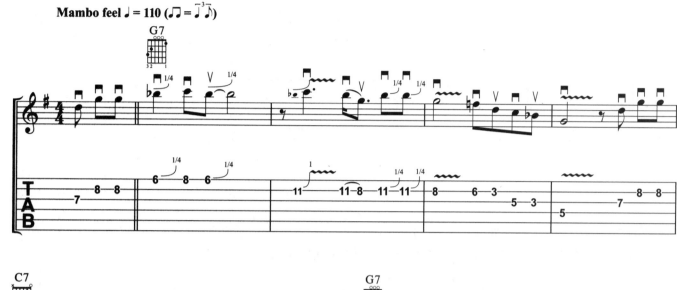

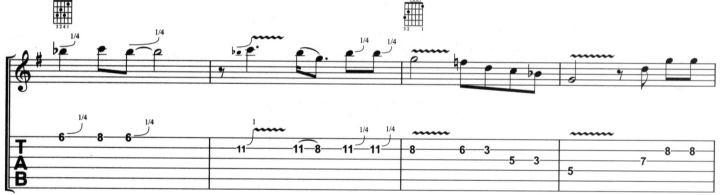

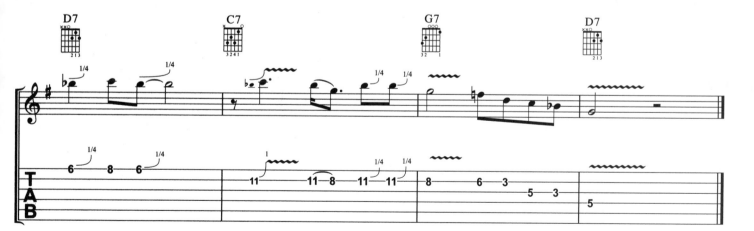

SOLO 2

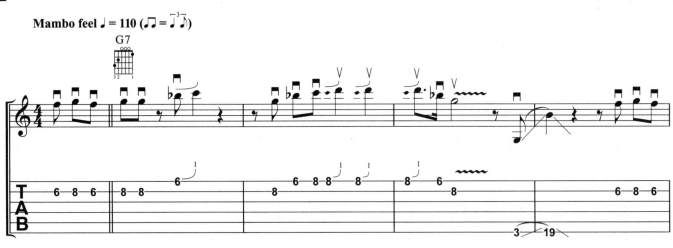

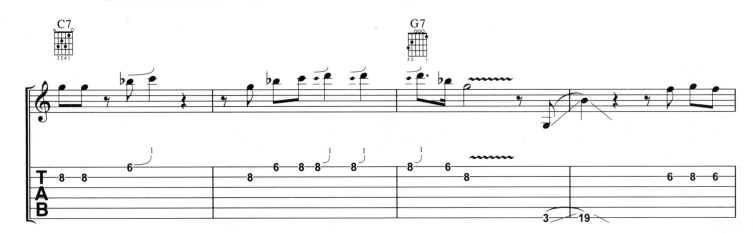

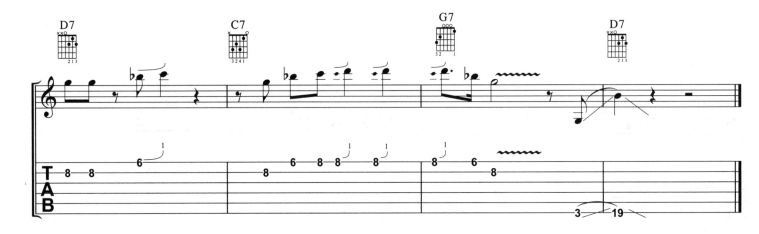

SOLO 3

Final Thoughts

Congratulations on completing *Alfred's Learn to Play Blues Guitar!* You can now play authentic blues rhythm and lead guitar like the pros. This isn't the end though—the blues is a life-long journey. Continue your studies by listening to, jamming, and absorbing as much blues music as you can. Best of luck in your musical journey!

About the Authors

Steve Trovato

Renowned educator Steve Trovato has authored over 30 instructional products covering all facets, levels, and styles of guitar playing. Steve is a full-time faculty member at the University of Southern California Thornton School of Music and graduated first in his class at the famed Guitar Institute of Technology, where he won the Gibson Award for outstanding musical achievement. In addition, he was inducted into the Tune-Up magazine hall of fame and has been featured in numerous guitar magazines, including *Guitar Player, Chitarre, Gitarre and Bass, Guitar World,* and *Just Jazz Guitar.*

Terry Carter

Terry Carter is a Los Angeles-based guitarist, songwriter, and producer. He has collaborated with Steve Trovato on various instructional books over the years and has published his own Rock Like the Pros series of books and online lessons. In addition, Terry has worked on projects with Weezer and the Ron Escheté Trio. His compositions can be heard on the MTV shows *Trippin', The Real World,* and *Wildboyz,* as well as on commercials for Puma. Terry owns and runs Carter's Coyote Pass Studios, a complete recording, mixing, and rehearsal studio.

Steve Trovato, on the right, with Terry Carter.